The Astrology of Serial Killers

VOLUME 1

By Rhys Navarro

The Astrology of Serial Killers Volume 1

ISBN: 9798524174277

©2021 Nysa Media, LLC

All rights reserved.
The content contained within this book may not be reproduced, duplicated or transmitted without direct written permission from the author or the publisher.

Under no circumstances will any blame or legal responsibility be held against the publisher, or author, for any damages, reparation, or monetary loss due to the information contained within this book, either directly or indirectly.

Legal Notice:
This book is copyright protected. It is only for personal use. You cannot amend, distribute, sell, use, quote or paraphrase any part, or the content within this book, without the consent of the author or publisher.

Disclaimer Notice:
Please note the information contained within this document is for educational and entertainment purposes only. All effort has been executed to present accurate, up to date, reliable, complete information. No warranties of any kind are declared or implied. Readers acknowledge that the author is not engaged in the rendering of legal, financial, medical or professional advice. The content within this book has been derived from various sources. Please consult a licensed professional before attempting any techniques outlined in this book.

By reading this document, the reader agrees that under no circumstances is the author responsible for any losses, direct or indirect, that are incurred as a result of the use of the information contained within this document, including, but not limited to, errors, omissions, or inaccuracies.

Natal charts created using Astrolog 7.10
http://www.astrolog.org/

Nysa Media
Los Angeles, CA
www.nysamedia.com

"You don't understand me. You are not expected to. You are not capable of it. I am beyond your experience."

– Richard Ramirez

Introduction	5
Chapter 1: Aries	12
Chapter 2: Taurus	29
Chapter 3: Gemini	43
Chapter 4: Cancer	59
Chapter 5: Leo	72
Chapter 6: Virgo	85
Chapter 7: Libra	101
Chapter 8: Scorpio	118
Chapter 9: Sagittarius	135
Chapter 10: Capricorn	157
Chapter 11: Aquarius	177
Chapter 12: Pisces	193
Conclusion	211
References	212

Introduction

Human society is maintained by a delicate arrangement of checks and balances. Occasionally that system "malfunctions," as in the case of serial killers. To restore balance, a realignment is necessary. The current method of restoring order is to remove the malfunctioning individual, by locking them away or eliminating them entirely. Either approach is an expensive cost to society.

If only there was a means by which to anticipate these murderous "glitches" ahead of time, then perhaps such breakdowns might be prevented and lives saved.

For millennia, astrology has been used to forecast the future and explain human behavior. Would it be possible to use this ancient tool to foresee the possibility of somebody turning into a serial killer before it occurs? Are there patterns or warning signs that astrology can help identify?

Astrology

The earliest recordings of lunar and stellar cycles appear to date back at least 25,000 years ago. Markings on bone, ivory, and cave walls have been found in numerous archeological explorations. At the start of the Neolithic era, when the hunter-gatherer way of life transitioned to a settled agricultural-based existence, it became important to forecast the raining, planting, harvesting, and winter periods. People began to track and record the movement and patterns of the sun, moon, planets, and stars *(Lindberg et al., 2003)*.

Physical observation of the influence of the moon and sun on natural phenomena, such as the tides, strengthened the belief that other heavenly bodies might similarly affect everyday life and occurrences.

Astrology as the discipline we know today can be attributed to the Greek and Hellenic periods. That knowledge was preserved and expanded during the Golden Age of Islam, with additions from India and even China. This Arabian system was later transmitted to Europe. At the start of the Renaissance, it merged with traditions that the Catholic church and monasteries had safeguarded, forming the basis of modern astrology *(Joanna Martine Woolfolk)*.

Astrology and astronomy were synonymous until the dawn of the Age of Enlightenment. In the sixteenth-and seventeenth centuries, observations and new theories from Galileo, Brahe, and Kepler slowly separated the disciplines. Eventually, astrology was discredited to the status of a pseudo-science.

Modern astrology is a body of knowledge thousands of years old that can describe personality traits and attitudes with finite accuracy. Astrology and psychology, doctrines of the study of human behavior, have much in common that should be explored.

It's easy to forget that natural phenomena we take for granted, such as the earth's magnetic field and the Van Allen belt, were only recently discovered in the last 100 to 200 years. These are energy zones that affect natural occurrences. What astrologers call the Zodiac is a similar energetic influence attributed to planets and other celestial objects. It is still awaiting full investigation and explanation *(Orion, 2020)*.

Astrology doesn't make us who we are. It's simply a mirror to help us see ourselves and our world more clearly. There will always be external forces - social, political, environmental - that shape our world. Astrology provides tools to help identify our potential strengths and weaknesses so we can better prepare to overcome life's challenges.

Serial Killers

Murderers who kill more than one person fall into three general categories: serial killers, spree killers, and mass murderers. *(Montaldo, 2004)*:

- A mass murderer usually kills as many people as possible in as short of time as possible in a limited geographical area. A school shooter would be an example of a mass murderer.

- A spree killer may commit many killings over a wide area, but the time duration is generally quite short, coming in spurts of activity. The Beltway Sniper is an example of a spree killer.

- Serial killers murder more than three people over a longer period of time with a break between the killings. These acts tend to be committed based on a psychological need that may follow a specific pattern.

The selection of killers included in this book fall within the third category.

The Zodiac

Many people associate the Zodiac with their sun sign, but it is only one component that makes up a full birth (or natal) chart. The Zodiac consists of 12 different signs arranged in a particular sequence *(Joanna Martine Woolfolk, 2013)*.

The alignment of the Zodiac signs with the sun, moon, and planets at the exact moment of a person's birth creates their unique celestial "fingerprint."

People exhibit various personality traits associated with their birth signs. These traits are further modified and influenced by the planets: not just the ruling planet for each Zodiac but other planets passing through specific signs, houses, and aspects.

Traits can be classified as either strengths or weaknesses, but the distinction isn't always so clear-cut. Strengths can become weaknesses if applied too aggressively, or to the detriment of other characteristics. Likewise, a weakness may become a positive if applied in the correct situation, or used to support or balance other personality traits.

For this book, each serial killers' natal chart has been summarized and generalized based on the influence of the planets in different signs, houses, and aspects. Only the major impacts and influences will be presented here.

Elements & Modalities

Each sign of the Zodiac represents one element - fire, water, earth, or air - as well as one modality defined as either cardinal, fixed, or mutable. *(Hewitt William W, 2016)*

Elements represent certain qualities and motivations assigned to groups of signs:

Fire Signs (*Aries, Leo, & Sagittarius*) - Active, competitive, and highly passionate; but can also become impatient and quick-tempered.

Earth Signs (*Taurus, Virgo, & Capricorn*) - Pragmatic, dependable, and realistic; but also known for being inflexible and ruthlessly stubborn.

Air Signs (*Gemini, Libra, & Aquarius*) - Prefers thinking logically rather than emotionally; but can also be indecisive and fickle.

Water Signs (*Cancer, Scorpio, & Pisces*) - Highly intuitive and naturally perceptive; but also prone to being moody and hypersensitive. Of the four elements, water is the most powerful and encompassing. It is fluid, flowing, and wavering. It has no shape or boundaries. It can conform to the other elements, or it can destroy them.

Modalities represent the manner in which these elemental qualities are expressed:

Cardinal Signs (*Aries, Cancer, Libra, and Capricorn*) - Visionaries, initiators, natural born leaders. They are action-oriented, goal-driven, and always in motion.

Fixed Signs (*Taurus, Leo, Scorpio, and Aquarius*) - Persistent, stable, reliable, and determined. They are intent on preserving the status quo and stubbornly resistant to change.

Mutable Signs (*Gemini, Virgo, Sagittarius, and Pisces*) - Flexible, changeable, adaptable, and suggestible. Good at multitasking, but often struggle with distractions.

Houses

The Zodiac is divided into 12 segments, or houses, each one ruled by a different sign. Starting with the rising (Ascendant) sign in the 1st house, the houses proceed counter-clockwise around the natal chart wheel.

Each house is associated with a different aspect of a person's life, such as:

1st House - Self, identity, attitude, approach to life
2nd House - Money, work, values, material possessions
3rd House - Communication, siblings, neighbors
4th House - Home, family, mother, children
5th House - Romance, love, creativity
6th House - Health, fitness, pets, service to others
7th House - Relationships, marriage, business partners
8th House - Death, inheritance, sex, debt, taxes
9th House - Travel, wisdom, philosophy, higher education
10th House - Career, reputation, fame, father, status
11th House - Groups, friends, technology, hope for the future
12th House - Endings, karma, solitude, afterlife

The rising sign and corresponding house positions are calculated using a person's birth time. For those serial killers whose actual time of birth is unknown, 12:00 noon will be used by default. A noon chart falls halfway through the day, representing a daily average for all the planetary positions. While not as precise, it still provides plenty of useful data.

Stellium

Some people's natal chart might include what astrologers call a *stellium*. A stellium occurs when a cluster of three or more planets appears in the same sign, and the house associated with that sign. This creates a laser-focused, hyper-concentration of energy in that aspect of a person's life *(Cunningham, 2011)*.

A stellium indicates where a person will devote their singular focus, often to an extreme. It intensifies those characteristics and themes, sharply defining a person's personality. Stelliums give a strong sense of a mission, drive, and purpose, a compulsion to accomplish their destiny.

While not negative per se, stelliums tend to dominate and "drown out" the rest of a person's chart. Because a stellium clumps the planets together, this leaves other sectors of the chart empty. Not investing time or energy into those areas can throw their life out of balance.

Stelliums also create vulnerabilities because so much is riding on one specific area. Temptations may arise to achieve that goal at all costs. Failure to succeed can be devastating. People with stelliums in their natal chart are prone to feeling alienated and alone, as there aren't many others who can relate to their intensity and focus.

Chapter 1: Aries

(March 21 - April 19)
Modality - Cardinal
Element - Fire

Aries Personality Traits

Some of the strengths associated with people born under the Zodiac sign Aries are:

- They are confident of their abilities and will succeed in any task that they undertake.

- They are courageous and not afraid to investigate unknown things.

- When new or unknown ideas, products, or services appear, they will be part of the early users or adopters.

- Aries personalities are dynamic and forceful.

- Aries people are perceptive and alert to the flow of life.

- When something interests them, they become very enthusiastic about it.

- They usually display a lot of energy.

- People with an Aries Zodiac sign like to explore and push existing boundaries.

However, Aries personalities can also exhibit the following weaknesses:

- They are volatile and can quickly lose their temper.

- Patience is not a virtue for an Aries personality.

- They can be impulsive and act without analyzing consequences.

- They tend to be selfish, ignoring the needs of other people.

- Aries personalities can be showoffs as they try to impress an audience.

- They can display recklessness and disregard for common sense.

Aries is one of the four <u>cardinal</u> signs of the Zodiac. The positive aspects of cardinal signs indicate ambitious, highly motivated individuals who take initiative. But when in excess, the cardinal energy can make an Aries impulsive, impatient, rude, aggressive, unfocused, and bored, with no energy to finish what they've started. They can come across as being disorganized and irresponsible, especially in relationships.

Aries also operates through its element, which is <u>fire</u>. Fire in Aries is akin to the initial combustion of a match, the spark that gives life to the creative process. The fire element is enthusiastic, volatile, creative, and forceful. But fire signs can also be selfish, arrogant, and feel threatened when they don't get their way. Fire in Aries must be controlled and managed to avoid excesses that can lead to negative behavior.

Aries Serial Killer 1: Keith Hunter Jesperson

Nickname: The Happy Face Killer

The nickname came from his habit of drawing smiley face ideograms on his letters to newspapers and law enforcement agencies.

Biography:

Keith Hunter Jesperson was born on April 6, 1955, in Chilliwack, Province of British Columbia, Canada *(Olsen, 2008)*.

His parents were Leslie and Gladys Jesperson, and Keith was the middle child with two brothers and two sisters on either side. He was treated as a pariah by his family and found it difficult to fit in because he was awkward and large for his age. His brothers nicknamed him Igor, shortened to Ig, a reference to the hunchback assistant in the 1931 movie *Frankenstein*.

The unfortunate nickname stuck throughout his school years, where he was teased and bullied by other children. As a result, he became a shy loner who played with himself most of the time.

Keith's father was a violent and domineering alcoholic who often abused his son. This included severe beatings and even electric shocks - often in front of other people. This only intensified Keith's withdrawal from normal contact and loving behavior.

Starting around the age of 5, Jesperson developed an unhealthy propensity for watching animals kill each other. He would capture birds and stray cats and dogs around the family's trailer park, torture them, then strangle them to death. These behaviors were early indications of psychological disorders and a tendency to commit acts of violence. He began to wonder how it would feel to conduct the same brutality against humans.

Jesperson's desire to hurt other people led to his first murder attempt at the age of 10. He violently beat a childhood friend and had to be separated by his father. His second attempt occurred about a year later at a public pool, in which he held another boy's head underwater until the lifeguard pulled him away. He also shot two people with a BB gun.

Jesperson graduated from school in 1973, but he did not attend college. He was very awkward with girls and did not have success in stable relationships until after graduation. In 1975, at the age of 20, he married a girl named Rose Hucke, and they had three children.

He worked as a truck driver to support his family. His wife began suspecting him of having extramarital affairs on the road. She left him and moved to Spokane, Washington in the United States, taking the children with her. After 15 years of marriage, the couple divorced in 1990.

In order to start a new life, Jesperson began training to join the Royal Canadian Mounted Policemen. A big man, Jesperson was 6'6" and weighed 240 pounds. During training, he injured himself in a fall and was permanently dismissed from the RCMP.

Losing his family and his dream job at the same time pushed Jesperson over the edge. He moved to Cheney, Washington and returned to driving trucks on long-haul, interstate routes.

His history of cruelty to animals, coupled with the nomadic life of a truck driver, made Jesperson realize he could get away with murder without being suspected.

Crime Review:

His first known murder was in 1990 near Portland, Oregon. He picked up Taunja Bennett in a bar and brought her home to the house he was renting. After she refused to have sex with him, he beat and suffocated her. He established an alibi by going back to the bar, making sure to converse with others before returning to dispose of the body.

Most of his victims were prostitutes or transients who were lured into his truck, where he would sometimes rape them before strangling them to death.

In all, Jesperson is known to have killed 8 women in multiple states along his route:

- *January 1990-* Portland, Oregon. Taunja Bennett, 23. She was punched in the face twenty times, raped, and strangled.

- *August 1992-* Blythe, California. Claudia (surname unrevealed). Raped and strangled.

- *September 1992-* Turlock, California. Cynthia Lyn Rose, 32. Strangled.

- *November 1992-* Salem, Oregon. Laurie Ann Pentland, 26. Strangled.

- *July 1993-* Santa Nella, California. Carla/Cindy (exact name and age unknown) Her manner of death is unknown.

- *September 14, 1994-* Crestview, Florida. Susanne, 40. Manner of death is unknown.

- *January 1995-* Spokane, Washington. Angela Surbrize, 21. She was raped, strangled, then dragged by a truck.

- *March 10, 1995-* Washougal, Washington. Julie Ann Winningham, 41. She was strangled.

Jesperson's final victim was his fiancé, whom he killed because he thought she was only interested in his money. He quickly became the prime suspect in her death. After two failed suicide attempts, he turned himself in to the police. He was arrested on March 30, 1995.

Jesperson later claimed to have committed up to 185 murders, but this cannot be confirmed. He is currently serving four life sentences.

His nickname came about through a bizarre series of events. After the murder of Taunja Bennett, a woman named Laverne Pavlinac confessed to the crime and implicated her abusive boyfriend, John Sosnovske. Her motive was a desire to get out of the relationship. They were both arrested and sentenced to 10 years in prison. No one believed Pavlinac when she claimed to have made the whole thing up.

With all the attention going to Pavlinic and Sosnovske, Jesperson wrote a confession on the bathroom wall of a truck stop and signed it with a smiley face. When that failed to garner any recognition, he penned lengthy letters to media outlets and police departments confessing to his murders. He signed each letter with a smiley face. The media dubbed him, "The Happy Face Killer."

Pavlinic and Sosnovske spent four years behind bars for a crime they didn't commit. It wasn't until Jesperson revealed previously unknown details of his killings that they were finally released.

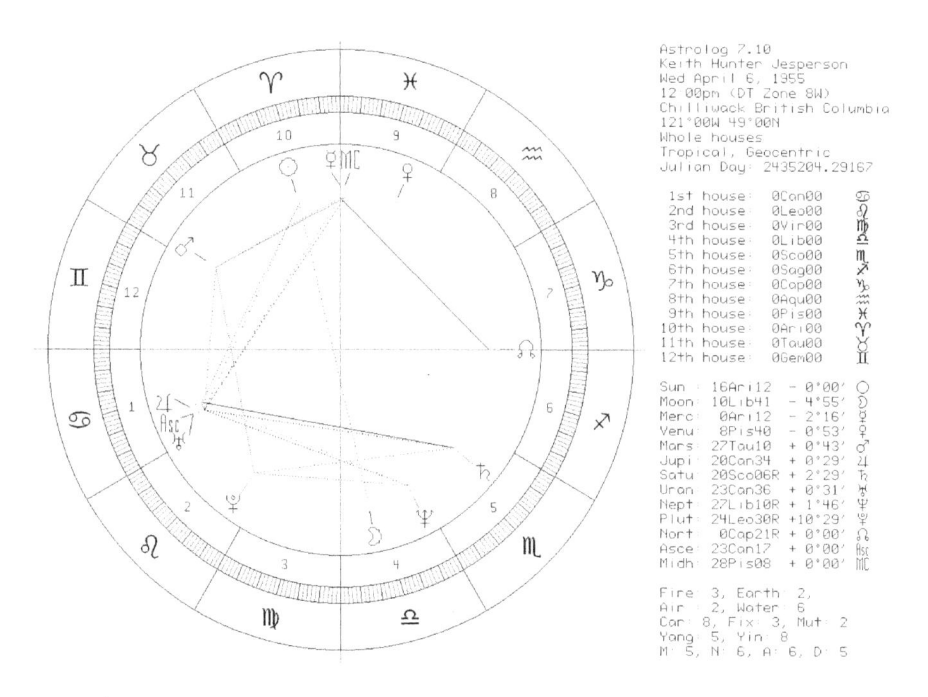

```
Astrolog 7.10
Keith Hunter Jesperson
Wed April 6, 1955
12:00pm (DT Zone 8W)
Chilliwack British Columbia
121°00W 49°00N
Whole houses
Tropical, Geocentric
Julian Day: 2435204.29167

1st house:  0Can00
2nd house:  0Leo00
3rd house:  0Vir00
4th house:  0Lib00
5th house:  0Sco00
6th house:  0Sag00
7th house:  0Cap00
8th house:  0Aqu00
9th house:  0Pis00
10th house: 0Ari00
11th house: 0Tau00
12th house: 0Gem00

Sun : 16Ari12  - 0°00'
Moon: 10Lib41  - 4°55'
Merc: 0Ari12   - 2°16'
Venu: 8Pis40   - 0°53'
Mars: 27Tau10  + 0°43'
Jupi: 20Can34  + 0°29'
Satu: 20Sco06R + 2°29'
Uran: 23Can36  + 0°31'
Nept: 27Lib10R + 1°46'
Plut: 24Leo30R +10°29'
Nort: 0Cap21R  + 0°00'
Asce: 23Can17  + 0°00'
Midh: 28Pis08  + 0°00'

Fire: 3, Earth: 2,
Air : 2, Water: 5
Car : 8, Fix : 3, Mut: 2
Yang: 5, Yin : 8
M: 5, N: 6, A: 6, D: 5
```

Keith Hunter Jesperson - April 6, 1955

19

Overview of Birth Chart

Planets and points in the signs

Sun in Aries- He tends to be a loner and are self-centered, concentrate on his interests, and are aggressive in relationships.

Moon in Libra- He is self-indulgent and can be passive-aggressive. He may attempt to co-opt others to do his will without being completely honest about his true agenda.

Mercury in Aries- He is opinionated and impulsive. Decisions are driven by the need for instant gratification. He can become aggressive when confronted with conflicting opinions and ideas.

Venus in Pisces- His natural emotional state of love and compassion has been distorted into cruelty to others. He may get lost in his own fantasy world and find the real world dull and boring.

Mars in Taurus- Once he has set his mind on a goal, he will pursue it with relentless dedication. He despises when things get in the way of his plans.

Jupiter in Cancer- His childhood emotional experiences will determine his emotional growth path as an adult. He lives in the past, to the point of appearing almost stuck in time. He is scared of change.

Saturn in Scorpio- Whatever he does, he will do it with intensity. He can be highly secretive. On the negative side, there is a risk of ruthlessness; he will do anything to get ahead. He can manipulate any situation to his advantage.

Discussion:

All the positive aspects of an Aries personality were twisted into negative qualities for Keith Jesperson. Due to the dominant influence of the Sun in Aries, his energies and passions were self-centered. His primary drive was unhealthy self-satisfaction and stimulation, reinforced by his dark experiences as a child.

Without knowing his birth time, it's hard to give an exact forecast. As such, his road to becoming a serial killer is not obvious from his chart. Perhaps a full reading in his youth might have pointed to the sinister scenario that was still preventable at that stage.

Aries Serial Killer 2: Paul John Knowles

Nickname: The Casanova Killer

He was called "Casanova" for his good looks and charming personality.

Biography:

Paul John Knowles was born on April 17, 1946, in Orlando, Florida, in the United States. His parents were Thomas Jefferson and Bonnie Knowles. His mother was one of the few people in his life that he truly loved *(Fawkes, 2004)*. The family lived in a 3-room house—a main room, one bedroom, and a kitchen. Their toilet was an outhouse.

The five Knowles children were all regularly abused by their father. According to his brother, Paul was nearly beaten to death more than once. He would run off into the woods until he'd healed, then come home until the next time.

At the age of 8, Knowles had already stolen a bike and committed various petty crimes. His father turned him over to the state, where he was placed in the notorious Dozier School for Boys. He stayed there off and on until his early teens.

Dozier was a reformatory known for its extreme brutality. Boys were severely beaten, raped, and sometimes even killed by guards. A state investigation that led to the school's closure in 2011 uncovered at least 81 child deaths at the hands of school employees. It's likely that Knowles' experience at Dozier turned him from a troubled kid into a hardened criminal and killer.

He was convicted and jailed for the first time at the age of 19. Afterward, he spent about six months of each year behind bars for robbery and auto theft. Somewhere during this period, he met and married Jackie Knight, but the marriage did not last.

While serving his sentence, Knowles began corresponding with a divorced waitress named Angela Covic. She visited him in jail and agreed to marry him. She even paid for lawyers to arrange his parole. Knowles was released in May 1974 and flew directly to San Francisco for the wedding. But a psychic warned Covic about a "very dangerous man" entering her life, so she called off the nuptials.

Crime Review:

Feeling angry and rejected, Knowles claims that the night Covic broke up with him, he went out and killed three people on the streets of San Francisco. This has not been verified.

He returned home to Jacksonville and was jailed after he stabbed a bartender in a bar fight. He picked the lock to his cell and escaped on July 26, 1974.

That night, Knowles embarked on a senseless four-month killing spree that left at least 20 people dead across 6 states. His victims had nothing in common with each other: they were men, women, and children; both gay and straight; ranging in age from 7 to 65. The only group excluded from his rampage were young boys. Even when they were present at killings, he left them untouched.

Here's a brief timeline of his crimes and the victims:

- *July 26*- Alice Cooper, 65. Gagged to death after he broke into her home and robbed her.

- *August 1*- Lillian and Mylette Anderson, 11 and 7. He strangled them and dumped their bodies in a swamp.

- *August 1*- Ima Jean Sanders, 13. Runaway from Texas who disappeared en route to Georgia to find her mother.

- *August 2*- Marjorie Howe, 49. He strangled her with a nylon stocking and stole her television set.

- *August 23*- Kathie Sue Pierce 22, In Georgia, Knowles broke into her home and strangled her with a phone cord, but left her 3-year-old son unharmed.

- *September 3*- William Bates, 23. Met Knowles at a roadside pub in Ohio. After some drinks, Knowles strangled him, dumped his body in the woods, and stole his car.

- *September 18*- Emmett and Lois Johnson, 60s. Victims were camping in Ely, Nevada, where Knowles bound and shot them. He stole their credit cards.

- *September 21*- Charlynn Hicks, 43. Her motorcycle broke down in Texas. He offered to help and instead abducted, raped, and strangled her.

- *September 29*- Ann Dawson, a beautician from Birmingham, Alabama. They travelled together for a few days, then he killed her and dumped her body in the Mississippi River. It was never recovered.

- *October 16-* Karen Wine and her 16-year-old daughter, Dawn. He broke into their Connecticut home and raped them both before strangling them.

- *October 18-* Doris Hovey, 53. He broke into the home of a Virginia woman and shot her with her husband's rifle.

- *In late October-* Knowles picked up two hitchhikers in Key West, Florida but, after being stopped for a traffic violation, let them go. He contacted his lawyer and handed over a taped confession. He then slipped out of town.

- *November 2-* Edward Hilliard and Debbie Griffin. The couple were hitchhiking around Macon, Georgia. His body was found in the nearby woods; hers was never recovered.

- *November 6-* Carswell Carr, 45, and Amanda Carr, 15. He befriended Carr in Georgia then, when invited to Carr's home, stabbed him to death with a pair of scissors, then strangled his daughter.

- *November 8-* Knowles picked up a British journalist named Sandy Fawkes and drove her around Florida for several days, but let her go. She later wrote a book about her experience.

- *November 11-* Knowles demanded sex at gunpoint from a friend of the journalist, but she escaped and notified the police.

- *November 16-* Trooper Charles Eugene Campbell, 35, and James Meyer. Knowles was recognized by Campbell, a Florida Highway Patrol officer. In the attempted arrest, Knowles managed to overpower

Campbell and took him hostage. Knowles then carjacked Meyer, a Delaware businessman who happened to be passing by. After driving his two hostages to a remote site, Knowles handcuffed them to a tree and killed them both with Campbell's gun.

Knowles tried to escape a police roadblock by ramming his car through the barricade. He slipped away but was shot in the foot. A massive manhunt ensued, involving multiple law enforcement agencies, dogs, and helicopters. Despite this, he managed to evade capture.

On November 17, Knowles was cornered by David Clark, a Vietnam War veteran armed with a shotgun. Knowles was finally arrested. In custody, Knowles claimed to be responsible for 35 murders, but only 20 were ever corroborated.

On December 18, Knowles was taken to identify the location of the murder weapon he used to kill Campbell and Meyer. Riding in the backseat, Knowles used a hidden paperclip to free his handcuffs. There was no screen in the car. Knowles was able to grab the sheriff's handgun and fire a round through his holster. From the passenger seat, Georgia Bureau of Investigation Agent Ronnie Angel fired three shots into Knowles' chest, killing him instantly.

Overview of Birth Chart

Planets and points in the signs

Sun in Aries- He is self-centered and everything he does is directed towards himself and his needs. He is energetic and quick to become angry.

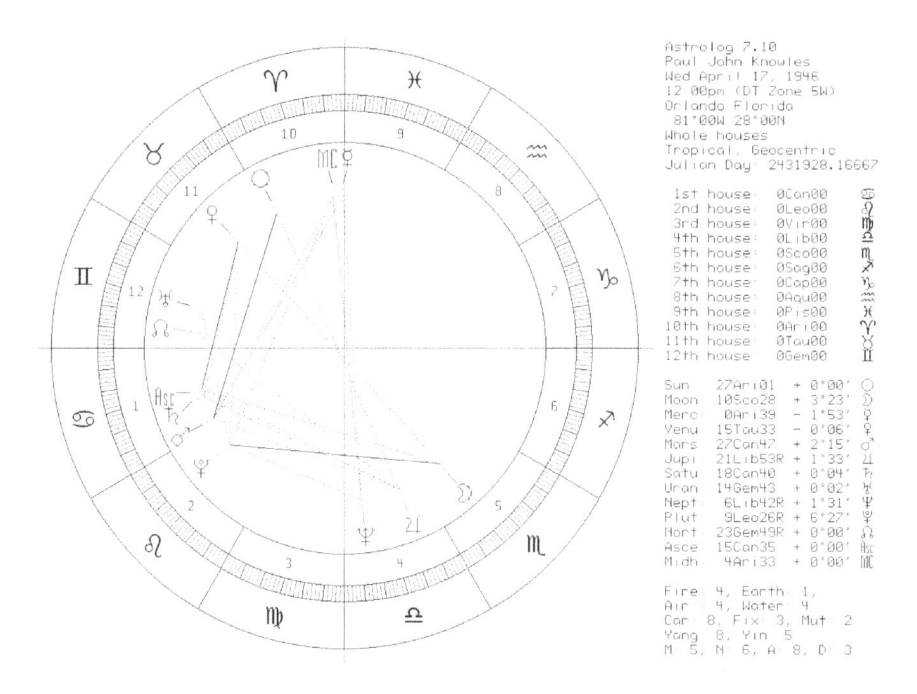

Paul John Knowles - April 17, 1946

Moon in Scorpio- He is secretive and inclined to brood in silence over wrongs done to him. He hates with a passion and will not forgive or forget past injuries. His moods are deep and extreme, and he pushes his reactions to the ultimate limit.

Mercury in Aries- He is filled with nervous energy and inclined to rash behavior. He grows bored quickly and needs constant stimulation.

Venus in Taurus- He is self-indulgent and needs to develop self-control. Highly possessive of romantic partners; any change in a relationship can throw his entire world into turmoil.

27

Mars in Cancer- He should beware of bottling his anger and holding grudges for a long time. He can become overly sensitive and inclined to lose control of his feelings.

Saturn in Cancer- His emotional security is very unstable because of his lack of love from at least one parent. His crippling insecurity makes him distrust others and feel very lonely and isolated. Prone to becoming obsessive.

Discussion:

Knowles exhibited all the negative attributes of Aries, impulsiveness, recklessness, temperamental. Coupled with the volatility of the element of fire, it led to disaster.

Given the background of abuse by his father and in the reformatory, all the warnings contained in his birth chart became a chilling reality.

Shared Pointers From the Natal Chart Reports

Both these killers share the Sun in Aries. All the positive aspects of an Aries personality were turned into negative traits for them. Their energies and interests were self-centered, their primary focus was unhealthy self-satisfaction, and stimulation which were reinforced by the other readings of their Zodiac.

Chapter 2: Taurus

(April 20 - May 20)
Modality - Fixed
Element - Earth

Taurus Personality Traits

Taurus personalities exhibit varying degrees of the following strengths:

- In all endeavors, they are persistent and will not give up.
- They are easygoing and not fazed by anything.
- They are loving and romantic in nature and also love the good things in life.
- They are determined, striving to accomplish whatever they set out to do.
- They highly value security.
- You can always rely on a Taurus to follow through with their commitments.
- They tend to be patient, not rushing anything.
- They are warm-hearted and love people and nature.

The following weaknesses can be expected from Taurus personalities:

- When taken to extremes, their loving nature can turn to jealousy.
- They may become resentful if they perceive something or someone is being unfair.

- They can become stubborn if they feel they are being manipulated or pushed into directions that they do not want to go.

- They are prone to becoming hedonistic.

- They may become obsessive about their favorite people and general situations.

- Their pursuit of the good things in life can lead to greed and hoarding.

- They are slow to anger but once enraged, like a bull, they will charge blindly.

Taurus is one of the <u>fixed</u> signs of the Zodiac. Fixed signs are known for being persistent and committed to their plans. When taken to excess, this determination turns into stubborn fixation and unwillingness to change.

An <u>earth</u> sign, Tauruses are no-nonsense, pragmatic, and focused on the material world. This sometimes leads them to become rigid, demanding, and harshly critical when things don't go as planned.

Taurus Serial Killer 1: David Copeland

Nickname: The London Nail Bomber

He planted and detonated three nail bombs that caused multiple deaths and serious injuries.

Biography:

David Copeland was born on May 15, 1976, in Hanworth, in the London Borough of Hounslow, to Stephen and Caroline Copeland. He was one of three brothers. Having an above-average IQ, David attended Yateley school where he did well. His teachers remember him as a sensitive and well-behaved child *(BBC News, 2000)*.

Exaggerated by his small build, David's development in his teenage years was slower than that of his schoolmates. His parents became worried about his sexual growth. When David was 13, they sent him to a doctor for a thorough examination, including a genital inspection. This embarrassing event left him with a deep resentment towards his parents.

At the age of 12, he started having sadomasochistic dreams of torturing women as slaves and fantasized about being reincarnated as an SS officer. Around this time, David also began to suspect he may be homosexual.

When David was 19 years old, his parents split up acrimoniously. This angered him to the extent that he cut off communications with his friends and family. He started drinking heavily and using heroin.

After leaving school in 1992, David blamed immigrants for his inability to find a job. These beliefs planted the early seeds of bigotry and racism. At the end of the 1990s, he left home to work on the underground in London. Not knowing the city, he spent his time after work sitting in his room or dallying with prostitutes.

He joined the right-wing British National Party (BNP), which campaigned against immigration. He later left them as they rejected violence.

During his time with the BNP, he came into contact with racial and right-wing revolutionary material from the internet, including *A Practical Guide to Aryan Revolution* by David Myatt. He taught himself how to construct bombs from *The Terrorist's Handbook*, which he downloaded from the internet.

After leaving the BNP, David joined the Neo-Nazi terrorist group, the National Socialist Movement, led by David Myatt. He became the regional leader for Hampshire shortly before his terror campaign.

Crime Review:

After a series of bombing attacks in Atlanta in the United States, David Copeland began to develop his own plans for a bombing campaign in England. He used Myatt's pamphlet as a source of inspiration. His goal was to start a racial war.

With knowledge he gleaned from the internet, Copeland constructed bombs using fireworks as explosives and alarm clocks as timers. Four-inch nails were packed around the entire device.

His first bomb detonated on April 19, 1999, outside a supermarket in Brixton, an area with a large black community. The blast sent hundreds of nails flying in all directions. 48 people were injured, several seriously.

On April 24, he planted a bomb in Brick Lane, in the East End of London, the center of a large Bengali area. A passerby found the sports bag containing the homemade device and put inside the trunk of his car for safe-keeping. While he was phoning the police about what he thought was lost property, the device exploded. 13 people were injured.

The final bomb, containing 1,500 nails, detonated on April 30 at a pub in the center of London's gay area. Because the bag was hidden under a table, the explosion resulted in serious leg injuries. 3 people were killed, 4 required amputations, 26 were severely burned, and another 53 badly injured.

Footage of David from a closed-circuit surveillance camera at the site of the Brixton bombing was widely televised. He was identified by a colleague and arrested by the police. He confessed at once to the bombings.

In his bedroom, Scotland Yard officers found two red-and-black Nazi flags hanging on a wall, as well as a collage of photos and newspaper stories from the bomb blasts.

During his trial, David was identified as schizophrenic but judged sane enough to accept responsibility for his deeds. He was sentenced to a minimum of 50 years in jail.

In 2021, he converted to Islam and now goes by the name "Saddam" in honor of the Iraqi dictator.

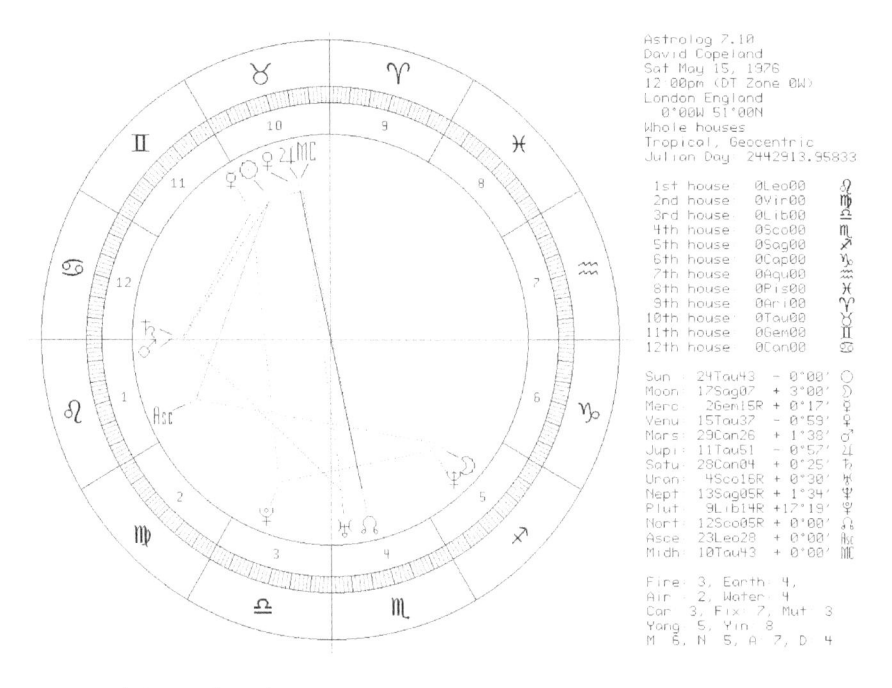

David Copeland - May 15, 1976

Overview of Birth Chart

Planets and points in the stars

Sun in Taurus- He is stubborn; it is not easy to change his opinions.

Moon in Sagittarius- Friendship means a lot to him but, on the negative side, he can be intolerant, close-minded, dogmatic, and arrogant.

Mars in Cancer- His moods are important to his well-being. If angered, he should try not to hold a grudge for a long time.

Stellium in Taurus (Sun, Venus, Jupiter)- He is old-fashioned and stubbornly resistant to change. He clings to out-dated ideas; maintaining the status quo is sacred to him. He is an immovable force; no amount of pressure can force him to do something he doesn't want to do.

Discussion:

Without an accurate birth time, we don't know for sure in which house David Copeland's Taurus stellium appears, but his stubborn adherence to old-fashioned, traditional values might have contributed to his racism and homophobia.

His childhood provides some clues that turned him into a calculated killer. The imagined slight of being a homosexual fueled his anger and bigotry. The strong ties to his mother were replaced with deep-seated anger when she abandoned him and his family.

The negative side of the Moon in Sagittarius manifested in the racial hatred and intolerance that lies at the core of his belief systems.

Taurus Serial Killer 2: Martha Beck

Nickname: The Lonely Hearts Killer

Martha Beck and her accomplice, Raymond Fernandez, murdered women they met through advertisements in magazines for people looking for love or friendship. These ads were known as *Lonely Hearts*.

Biography:

She was born Martha Jule Seabrook on May 6, 1920, in Milton, Florida, in the United States. Her parents were William and Julia Seabrook. William was a weak man; unable to tolerate his domineering wife, he left his family when Martha was 10 years old. *(Fuchs, 1996)*.

Due to a glandular disorder, Martha was obese and not very pretty. When she was 26, she weighed over 300 pounds. She developed sexual desires at the age of 9 and had an early transformation to womanhood. Martha claimed she was raped by her brother, but her mother beat her for it, saying Martha was the one responsible.

Martha's mother also ridiculed her for being overweight. At school, her classmates relentlessly bullied and teased her. As a teenager, Martha ran away from home and joined the circus.

Martha completed her studies and graduated as a nurse in 1942. Her first medical job was an undertaker's assistant, preparing female bodies for burial. She moved to California and worked in an Army hospital, where she became pregnant. When the father refused to marry her, she returned home to Florida.

To avoid the stigma of being an unwed mother, Martha claimed her daughter's father was a serviceman who had died in the war. She later met, became pregnant, and married Alfred Beck, a bus driver, but the couple divorced six months later.

In 1946, she got a job at the Pensacola Hospital for Children. As a single mother with two young children, Martha escaped into a fantasy world of romance novels and movies. She met Raymond Fernandez through an ad in a *Lonely Hearts* magazine. Martha was immediately smitten.

Crime Review:

Raymond Fernandez was a seasoned criminal who specialized in meeting women through advertisements in *Lonely Hearts* magazines. He would woo them with romantic letters, then once they met in person, seduce them and steal their money. He stayed with Martha a few days before determining that she had nothing worth stealing, so he returned to New York.

Madly in love, Martha abandoned her children and followed Raymond back to New York. There she learned the nature of his business and proposed a partnership. She would play the role of Raymond's sister to help win over reluctant victims.

Starting in 1947, they preyed on lonely women for two years. Martha was very jealous and ensured Raymond did not have sexual relations with any of their victims.

The first murder for which they were convicted occurred when Martha caught Raymond in bed with Janet Fay. She smashed Fay's head with a hammer, then Raymond strangled her. They buried her body in the cellar of a rented house and covered it with fresh cement.

The couple then went to Grand Rapids, Wyoming where Raymond's next mark was waiting for them - a 28-year-old widow, Delphine Dowling, and her two-year-old daughter. Wedding plans were made.

On February 28, 1949, Dowling and Raymond got into an argument, so he gave her a dose of sleeping pills. The daughter, seeing her mother in a drugged stupor, started crying. Panicked, Martha choked her but didn't kill her.

Worried how Downing would react to the girl's bruises, Raymond shot her while she was still unconscious. Martha drowned the child in a basin of water. They buried both bodies in the basement, once again covering them with concrete.

Concerned neighbors reported the Downings' disappearance. The police arrived at the house, found the freshly poured concrete floor, and soon arrested the two killers.

Martha and Raymond were extradited to New York, which had the death penalty. Because of the scandalous nature of the crimes, the trial was a media sensation. Martha dramatically kissed Raymond in the courtroom, leaving his face smeared with lipstick.

Martha and Raymond were both convicted of the murder of Janet Fay and sentenced to death. They were electrocuted on the same day, March 8, 1951.

"My story is a love story. But only those tortured by love can know what I mean."
- Martha Beck

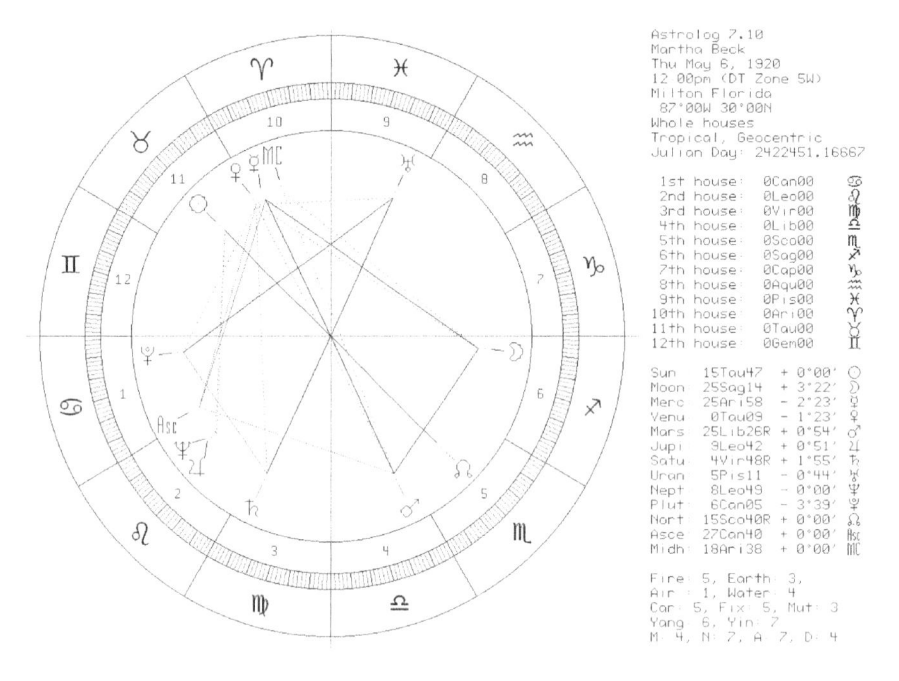

Martha Beck - May 6, 1920

Overview of Birth Chart

Planets and points in the stars

Sun in Taurus- She is slow to anger but will hold grudges for a long time. She has a fear of loss that is accompanied by jealousy and possessiveness.

40

Moon in Sagittarius- She has great friendships. On the negative side, she is intolerant, close-minded, arrogant, and risk-taking.

Mercury in Aries- She tends to be single-minded and only see things from her own standpoint. She makes quick, firm decisions, but fails to think things through properly, so her judgments can be short-sighted and ill-advised.

Venus in Taurus- She tends to form long-lasting relationships but are very jealous and possessive.

Jupiter in Leo- She has a brazen, take-charge attitude. She can be fanatical, self-centered, and impulsive. She is flamboyant and enjoys showing off.

Discussion:

Many of Martha Becks' problems can be traced back to her childhood when she was abused, unable to form the loving family attachments that are core attributes for Taurus. She valued her sexual relationship with Raymond more than her children, so she was willing to give them up rather than risk losing him.

Shared Pointers From the Natal Chart Reports

Martha Beck and David Copeland share both the Sun and Venus in Taurus, and Moon in Sagittarius. They are both self-centered. Their actions later in life indicate they were trying to find a substitute for the deprivations they were subjected to at an early age.

Chapter 3: Gemini

(May 21 - June 20)
Modality - Mutable
Element - Air

Gemini Personality Traits

The general strengths of Geminis are:

- They are adaptable and can change to fit in with many different scenarios.

- They are lively, light-hearted, and carefree.

- Geminis tend to be youthful and have young ideas, even when they are advanced in age.

- Flexibility is a key attribute of Geminis. They can accommodate many scenarios in their daily environment.

- Geminis are expressive and good communicators.

- They are intellectually curious and interested in learning about life in general.

- Geminis express themselves with eloquence and clear definition.

- They are humorous and witty.

They tend to exhibit the following weaknesses:

- Represented by the image of the twins, Geminis can have multiple sides, or hidden personas.

- They may have rapid and unpredictable mood swings.

- They are nervous, anxious, and indecisive.

- They can be superficial and avoid going into details.

- They jump between solutions without deciding what to do. This leads to inconsistent behaviors.

- They can be inquisitive to the point where it becomes a liability.

- To satisfy and support their positive attributes, they can resort to devious and crafty methods.

- Geminis have tense personalities and may be high-strung and nervous.

<u>Mutable</u> signs such as Gemini are the chameleons of the Zodiac, readily adapting to any new person or situation. But they can also be scattered, difficult to pin down, and easily led astray.

As an <u>air</u> sign, Geminis are generally sociable, adept and well-liked. But the air of Gemini is like a fast, swirling wind. When taken to extremes, these qualities can lead them to become unpredictable, emotionally detached, insensitive, and indecisive. Don't get too comfortable because they can change in the blink of an eye.

Combining both mutable and air means Gemini is the best connector of people and situations. Air gives Gemini the ability to communicate thoughts and ideas, while mutability keeps Gemini busy gathering and circulating information.

Gemini Serial Killer 1: Jeffrey Dahmer

Nickname: The Milwaukee Cannibal

He dismembered his victims and frequently ate some of their body parts.

Biography:

Jeffrey Dahmer was born on May 21, 1960, in Milwaukee, Wisconsin, in the United States. His parents were Lionel Herbert Dahmer and Joyce Annette Dahmer. He had one younger brother *(Dvorchak & Holewa, 1992)*.

Dahmer was a happy toddler, but a double hernia operation at the age of 4 led to a loss of confidence. He turned into a very subdued child. His father, who was a student pursuing a degree in chemistry, was frequently away for long periods of time. His mother became a hypochondriac and demanded constant attention from her husband. Neither parent devoted much time to their son who suffered from child abandonment syndrome, leading to psychological damage.

Around the age of 12, Dahmer grew fascinated with dead animals and began collecting their bones. He would bike along rural roads looking for roadkill to dissect to see how the body parts were connected. From his father, he acquired the knowledge to bleach bones and preserve them.

In high school, Dahmer became an outcast and started abusing alcohol. His grades declined and his parents' marriage fell apart. They divorced in 1978. During puberty, Dahmer discovered he was gay. He began fantasizing about controlling a submissive male; later his fantasies including dissecting his partners.

After his parents separated, Dahmer lived alone in the family house.

Crime Review:

He committed his first murder just after graduating in 1978, when he picked up a hitchhiker and lured him to his house with promises of drinks. At the house, he bludgeoned the person and then strangled him. He dismembered the corpse and buried it in the yard. He later exhumed the remains, dissolved the flesh, and crushed the bones before getting rid of the evidence.

In 1978, he attended Ohio University but dropped out after one semester due to his alcohol abuse. His father forced him to enlist in the US Army, where he served as a combat medic in Germany from 1979 to 1981. After several brushes with the law, his father sent him to stay with his grandmother in West Allis, Wisconsin.

Dahmer lived with his grandmother from 1981 until September 1988. During this period, he spent time at gay bathhouses, where he started drugging men and raping them while they were unconscious. After a few instances, he was denied access to all the establishments, but was never charged for the rapes.

He committed his second murder on November 20, 1987. He picked up a 25-year-old man in a bar and took him to a hotel room, where they had sex. According to Dahmer's testimony, he woke up with the body of the man beneath him. He used a large suitcase to transport the corpse to his grandmother's house, where he dissected the remains after a week and disposed of the small parts in normal trash bags.

In 1988, Dahmer spent 10 months in prison for groping a 13-year-old boy and offering the child money for nude photos. After his release, Dahmer began killing in earnest.

He established a routine for each of his murders. He would render the victim unconscious and, after or before having sex with that person, he would kill them in various ways, mostly strangulation or injection. He would dismember the body and retain portions for eating or as souvenirs. He always preserved their skulls and genitalia. He developed rituals and experimented with drilling into their skulls while they were still alive, injecting them with muriatic acid. He was sexually attracted to corpses and performed sexual acts with them.

From 1988 to 1991, Dahmer killed 15 men and boys. He carefully selected victims from the fringes of society, which made their disappearances less noticeable and his own capture less likely.

On May 27, 1991, Dahmer's neighbor called to report an Asian boy running naked in the street. When the police arrived, Dahmer claimed the boy was his 19-year-old lover. In fact, the boy was only 14 years old. The police believed Dahmer and escorted the boy back to his home. Dahmer proceeded to kill him.

He was finally caught on July 22nd, 1991, a 32-year-old African American man named Tracy Edwards was found wandering the streets with handcuffs hanging from his wrist. Edwards claimed Dahmer had drugged him and attempted to restrain him, but he managed to escape.

Upon arriving at Dahmer's apartment, the police found damning evidence, including photos, human heads, and other body parts stored in his refrigerator. Even though Dahmer had been on probation during this time, his parole officer never checked on his home. His gruesome collection had gone undiscovered for years.

Dahmer was sentenced to life imprisonment. On November 28th, 1994, he was clubbed to death by a fellow inmate.

"The killing was a means to an end. That was the least satisfactory part. I didn't enjoy doing that. That's why I tried to create living zombies with uric acid in the drill [to the head], but it never worked. No, the killing was not the objective. I just wanted to have the person under my complete control, not having to consider their wishes, being able to keep them there as long as I wanted."
- Jeffrey Dahmer

Overview of Birth Chart

Planets and points in the signs

Sun in Gemini– He is emotionally detached and exhibits a lack of concentration and fickleness. He tends to live in your head.

Moon in Aries– He tends to be overconfident, aggressive, and harsh. He becomes aggressive over even small things and won't hesitate to show his temper.

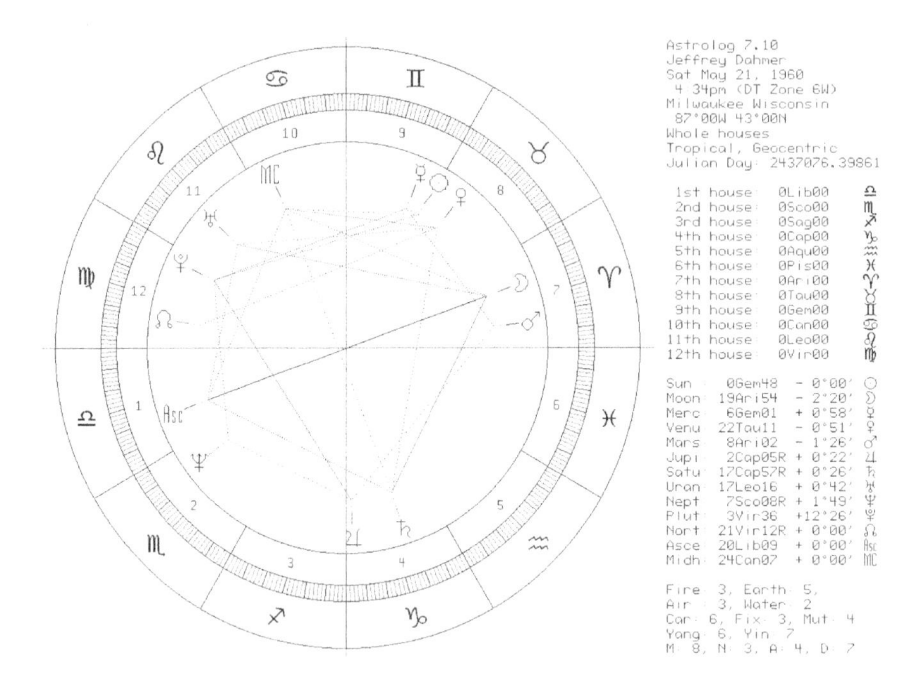

Jeffrey Dahmer - May 21, 1960

Venus in Taurus– He needs outside stimulants to get his sexuality in gear.

Mars in Aries– The tendency to do things in new creative ways is very strong.

Scorpio in Neptune- He finds pleasure in dark places. He is prone to addiction and alcoholism.

Planets and points in the houses

Venus in the 8th house– His sex life is unconventional. He oversteps propriety borders, including things which are forbidden or taboo.

Pluto in the 12th house– He has obsessive and compulsive tendencies. He lives in his own fantasies, trying to escape the reality of his own pain.

Discussion:

Jeffrey Dahmer already started showing signs of his derangement at a young age. The lack of parental involvement reinforced the attributes seen with the planets and points in the signs and houses.

His addictive tendencies, dark obsessions, sexual taboos, and escapist fantasies all speak to the demented character Dahmer ultimately became.

Gemini Serial Killer 2: David Berkowitz

Nickname: Son of Sam

He named himself in letters to the police and media.

Biography:

David Berkowitz was born Richard David Falco on June 1st, 1953, in New York, in the United States. His birth and subsequent adoption history played an enormous role on his development and personality. His mother was Elizabeth Broder, who first married Tony Falco, but the marriage did not last.

David's biological father was Joseph Klineman but his mother registered his birth under her husband's name. When only a few days old, David was adopted by a childless Jewish couple, Nathan and Pearl Berkowitz, who changed his name to David Richard Berkowitz (*Klausner, 1981*).

Despite the love and affection he received from his adoptive parents, David had a troubled childhood. He lost interest in schooling and education at an early age and started stealing and setting fires. His adoptive mother died when he was 14. Her death devastated him, as he loved her very much.

In 1971, at the age of 17, David joined the United States Army and served in the USA and South Korea. After his discharge, he located his biological mother, and she disclosed the details of his birth and adoption.

The revelation shattered David's sense of identity, especially when it came to reluctant father figures. Some psychologists have stated the major cause of his mental issues was related to his feelings of rejection by his biological parents.

Crime Review:

During the mid-1970s, David started committing violent crimes. He claims to have stabbed two women with a hunting knife on Christmas Eve, 1975, although police never linked him to that attack.

David's first confirmed shooting was in July 1976, when he shot two women sitting in their car in the Bronx area of New York. One was killed instantly, but the other survived.

So began the Son of Sam's crime spree throughout the boroughs of New York City:

- *July 29, 1976-* The Bronx. Donna Lauria, 18 (killed) and Jody Valenti, 19 (wounded). David fired five shots into their car. Donna was shot in the neck and the arm, and died on the scene. Jody was shot in the thigh.

- *October 23, 1976-* Queens. Carl Denaro, 20 (wounded) and Rosemary Keenan, 18 (uninjured). Five shots were fired into their car. Carl was hit in the back of his skull but survived.

- *November 27, 1976-* Queens. Donna DeMasi, 16 (wounded) and Joanne Lomino, 18 (wounded). The girls were sitting on the front steps and tried to run inside when David began shooting at them. Donna was shot through the base of the neck. Joanne was shot in the lower spine and paralyzed.

- *January 30, 1977–* Queens. Christine Freund, 26 (killed) and John Diel, 30 (uninjured). The couple had just left a bar and gotten into their car when the windows shattered. Christine was shot in the head.

- *March 8, 1977–* Queens. Virginia Voskerichain, 19 (killed). She was walking home when she was shot in the head. She died instantly.

- *April 16, 1977–* Bronx. Valentina Suriani, 18 (killed) and Alexander Esau, 20 (killed). They were sitting in their car when David opened fire. Two bullets struck Valentina in the skull, killing her instantly. Two more hit Alexander in the head. A taunting letter was left at the crime scene addressed to the police, signed "The Son of Sam."

- *April 30, 1977–* Another letter from The Son of Sam was sent to the New York Daily News.

- *June 26, 1977–* Queens. Salvatore Lupo, 20 (wounded) and girlfriend Judy Placido, 17 (wounded). The couple was shot while sitting in their car. Salvator's wrist was shattered. Judy was hit in the shoulder and head, but the bullet did not penetrate her skull.

- *July 31, 1977–* Brooklyn. Bobby Violante, 20 (wounded) and Stacy Moskowitz, 20 (killed). The couple was shot in their car. Stacy was killed and Bobby was left permanently blind.

Another couple witnessed the last attack. A partial registration number of the car driven by the killer was recovered from the scene. Berkowitz was arrested on August 10, 1977.

During questioning, Berkowitz claimed his neighbor's dog spoke to him and demanded the blood of young girls. He underwent numerous psychological evaluations but was declared competent to stand trial. He later retracted his possessed dog story claiming, "it was all a silly hoax."

In 1978, Berkowitz pled guilty to the six killings, as well as nearly 1,500 fires he had set in and around New York City. He received 25-years-to-life for each murder. Upon hearing the judge's decision, Berkowitz tried to jump out of a window of the seventh-floor courtroom.

During the mid-1990s, Berkowitz claimed he had been a member of a violent Satanic cult and that his crimes were actually ritual murders. A new investigation began in 1996, but was suspended after the findings were inconclusive. Berkowitz remains the only person ever charged with the shootings.

"I was literally singing to myself on my way home, after the killing. The tension, the desire to kill a woman had built up in such explosive proportions that when I finally pulled the trigger, all the pressures, all the tensions, all the hatred, had just vanished, dissipated, but only for a short time."

-- David Berkowitz

Overview of Birth Chart

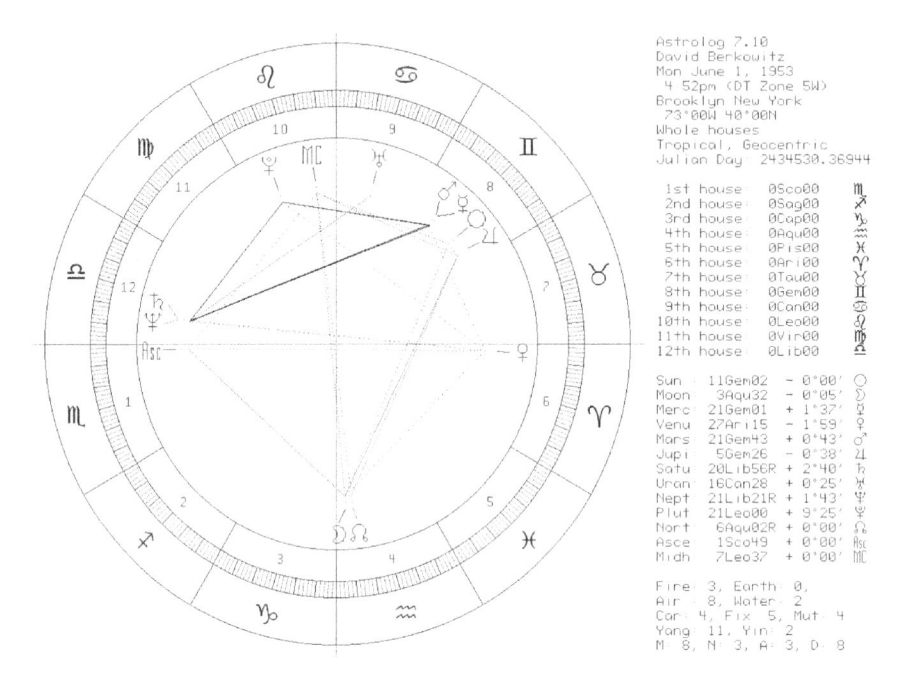

David Berkowitz - June 1, 1953

Planets and points in the signs

Scorpio rising– He can be highly suspicious and prone to paranoia. He may be manipulative, aggressive, destructive, violent, and cruel.

Sun in Gemini– He is emotionally detached.

Moon in Aquarius– He can be impersonal, stubborn, and lack compassion. He takes pride in going against the grain.

Venus in Aries– He can be inconsiderate and selfish.

56

Pluto in Leo- He can be self-centered and throw a tantrum when things don't go his way.

Stellium in Gemini (Sun, Mercury, Mars, Jupiter)- He has a dual nature and two distinct (often contradictory) personalities. He is restless and craves constant change. He gets bored easily which can get him into trouble. He enjoys talking but isn't always truthful.

Planets and points in the houses

Moon in the 4th house- He is insecure and prone to constant mood swings. Home and family are of great importance to him, especially his relationship with his father.

Stellium in the 8th house - He seeks power and control. He has an innate knowledge of life's deeper, darker subjects. He feels compelled to explore the macabre, taboo, and darker side of society. He may be a loner, rejected by society.

Saturn in the 12th house- He feels the need for isolation and may engage in secret activities. He is tormented by feelings of guilt. He may have lingering fears or phobias from childhood.

Neptune in the 12th house- He finds it hard to fit in and is detached from reality. He prefers to live in his own world.

Discussion:

The birth chart of David Berkowitz is dominated by the stellium in his 8th house of sex, death, and forbidden knowledge. The moon in his 4th house of family could explain why the rejection of his birth parents had such a profound negative impact on him.

When viewed as a whole, his chart shows many details that can be interpreted as an indication of the path that his life would take. The stellium in Gemini amplifies the negative traits normally associated with that sign - including emotional detachment, selfishness, and the need to digest experiences with resentment.

Shared Pointers From the Natal Chart Reports

The killers share a pointer in the Sun in Gemini. They are both detached, self-centered, inconsistent, highly strung. Above all, they both demonstrate the main Gemini trait of shifting moods at the drop of a hat.

Chapter 4: Cancer

(June 21 - July 22)
Modality - Cardinal
Element - Water

Cancer Personality Traits

The strengths identified with Cancer personalities are:

- They rely on intuition and react instinctively to situations.
- They do not hide their emotions.
- Creativity and the use of their imagination is a strongly developed trait.
- In business dealings, they tend to be astute, perceptive, and are not easily hoodwinked.
- They exhibit loving and caring natures.
- They are good at safeguarding physical property and relationships.
- Before making a decision, they will use a careful approach and weigh the merits of each solution.
- In line with their loving character, they are also supportive and sympathetic.

As a foil to their strengths, Cancers are also prone to certain weaknesses:

- They can be temperamental and moody.
- They tend to become over-excited and frenzied in their reaction to different occurrences.
- They cling to outdated perceptions, relationships, and ideas.

- Their disposition is erratic and can change quickly.

- They can be thin-skinned and react to any perceived criticism or slight.

- Due to their cautious nature, they find it hard to let go of anything.

Cancer is the sign of <u>cardinal</u> <u>water</u>. The water of Cancer is similar to that of a stream winding its way toward a pond or river. Cancers are emotional, understanding, and supportive. But true to their cardinal modality, Cancer's emotions are fast moving, can erupt unexpectedly, and are subject to change.

Cancers focus more on the internal home, family areas, and emotional feelings. There is a tendency for Cancers to go overboard with their emotional side. They are the most empathetic of the water signs.

Cancer Serial Killer 1: Robert Maudsley

Nickname: The Brain Eater or Hannibal the Cannibal

He was alleged to have eaten part of the brain of one of his victims, but that was subsequently shown to be untrue.

Biography:

Robert Maudsley was born on June 26, 1953, in Speke on the outskirts of Liverpool. He had eleven siblings. His parents were George and Jean Maudsley. Soon after his birth, the children were removed and placed in a Catholic orphanage *(Rickall, 2007).*

After spending nine years in the orphanage, the children were returned home to their parents. There they were repeatedly beaten and abused. Their father was a violent alcoholic, but many of the beatings were also instigated by their mother, who had an equally vicious and abusive nature.

The abuse scarred Robert to the extent that he remarked that he should have killed his parents before the experience twisted his mind. After complaints from the neighbors, Robert was placed in foster care.

At the age of 16, he ran away to London. He started using drugs and became a male prostitute to support his drug habit. After several suicide attempts, he sought psychiatric help.

Crime Review:

In 1974, Maudsley was picked up by John Farrell for sex. Farrell showed him pictures of children that he had abused sexually. In response, Maudsley strangled Farrell. He voluntarily turned himself over to the police. He was sent to Broadmoor Hospital, as he was deemed to be not accountable for his crime and unfit to stand trial.

In 1977, Maudsley and a fellow prisoner tortured convicted child molester, David Francis, to death over a period of nine hours. Maudsley was convicted of manslaughter and his sentence was changed to life imprisonment. He was sent to Wakefield prison.

In 1978, Maudsley killed two prisoners in one day: Sainey Darwood, who was serving time for killing his wife, and Bill Roberts, a child molester.

In 1983, it was decided Maudsley was too dangerous to keep in the general prison population. He was confined to a solitary cell in the basement of Wakefield prison. He is only allowed out for one hour per day and is escorted at all times by at least four prison officers.

Overview of Birth Chart

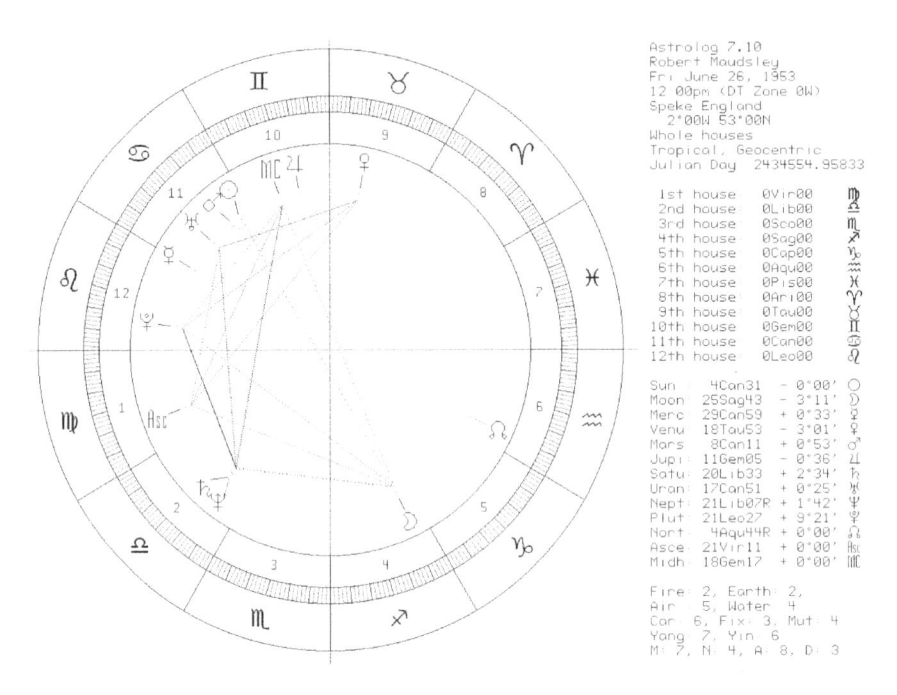

Robert Maudsley - June 26, 1953

Planets and points in the signs

Sun in Cancer– He responds to life through his emotions rather than through his mind. He has vivid and long-enduring memories of the past.

Moon in Sagittarius– He gets disappointed if his high expectations are not met. He can become intolerant and close-minded.

Mercury in Cancer– His mind is connected with his memories, feelings, and emotions from the past. He becomes

64

depressed over his problems. His emotions tend to rule his thought processes. He has difficulty seeing life objectively.

Mars in Cancer- His moods are very important to his overall well-being. He is easily angered whenever he thinks someone has slighted him.

Uranus in Cancer - He tends to have dramatic reactions and sudden mood shifts. He feels no one understands him. He may become insecure and retreat into his shell.

Stellium in Cancer (Sun, Mercury, Mars, Uranus)- He is hypersensitive, very emotional, and easily hurt by actions and words. Few people feel things as strongly as he does. He is highly protective of children.

Discussion:

Cancer is considered an unusual sign for a serial killer, because they are usually the nurturing caregivers of the Zodiac. Maudsley's stellium in Cancer takes those positive traits to the extreme, turning him into a vigilante protector of children. Had he been shown more compassion as a child, his life might have taken a very different course. Due to his own brutal childhood, he snaps every time he is confronted with a child abuser.

Cancer Serial Killer 2: Donato Bilancia

Nickname: The Monster of Liguria, also The Killer on the Trains

The nicknames were coined by the inhabitants of the Italian Riviera.

Biography:

Donato Bilancia was born on July 10, 1951, in the city of Potenza in southern Italy. The names of his parents and any siblings are not known. The family moved to the north of Italy when Donato was 5 years old and settled in Genoa *(Montolli, 2017)*.

The slow disintegration of his parents' marriage resulted in an unhappy childhood. His father beat him regularly, and Donato blamed himself for their marital troubles.

These issues led to him wetting his bed until he was 12 years old. Physical conditions can cause chronic bedwetting but, for Donato, it was likely the result of stress. His mother would put his urine-soaked mattress on the balcony for all to see, further damaging his self-esteem.

Compounding the problem was the fact Donato had a small penis. When undressing him for bed, his aunt would pull down his underwear in front of his cousins to make fun of his underdeveloped penis. Later in life, that shame and hate would be reinforced by prostitutes who also ridiculed his penis size.

At the age of 14, Donato dropped out of school and supported himself by taking odd jobs, such as bartender and delivery boy.

While still a teenager, Donato was arrested for stealing a scooter and a truck loaded with sweets. In 1974, he was sentenced to prison for possessing an illegal firearm.

Over the next few years, he was constantly in and out of jail for committing a series of robberies in both France and Italy. Donato was also a compulsive gambler.

Crime Review

Until late in his forties, Donato did not have a record of violent behavior. His killing spree was triggered by a friend's betrayal. The friend, aware of Donato's compulsive gambling addiction, tricked him into playing in a rigged card game where he lost over $200,000.

When Donato learned of the double-cross, he strangled his friend, shot the man who rigged the game, and shot the man's wife. Donato would later testify these killings gave him a taste for murder.

Donato was not a typical serial killer with a fixed methodology. The randomness of his attacks made it difficult for the police to link the crimes to a single suspect.

His victims, starting in October 1997, were:

- The friend, the crooked card dealer, and his wife. Donato emptied their safe afterward.

- He followed a jeweler home to rob him. When the man's wife began screaming, Donato shot them both dead and stole all the jewelry in their safe.

- He robbed and murdered a money-changer.

- Two months later, Donato murdered a night watchman, simply because he despised night watchmen.

- He murdered an Albanian prostitute.

- He killed a Russian worker.

- He robbed and a second money-changer and killed him, shooting him several times.

- In March 1998, he forced a prostitute to give him oral sex at gunpoint. Two night watchmen tried to intervene; he shot and killed them both. He then shot the prostitute. She survived and helped the police identify him.

- He killed a Nigerian prostitute.

- He killed a Ukrainian prostitute.

- He robbed and assaulted an Italian prostitute but did not kill her.

- In April 1998, on a train from Genoa to Venice, he followed a young woman to the toilet. He unlocked the bathroom door with a skeleton key, shot her in the head, and stole her train ticket. Later he testified that he just wanted to kill a woman.

- Six days later, on the train to Sanremo, he broke in on another woman on the toilet and shot her, using her jacket as a silencer.

- His last killing happened on April 20, 1998. He robbed and shot a gas station attendant.

At this point, police had a description of his black car, an Identikit, as well as DNA samples. After following Donato for a couple of days and collecting DNA from various items he used, investigators were able to match his DNA to DNA found at the crime scenes.

The worst serial killer in Italian history was arrested on May 6, 1998. His killing spree lasted only seven months, from October 1997 to April 1998, but during that time he murdered 17 people. He was sentenced to 13 life sentences.

Donato Bilancia died from COVID-19 in December 2020.

Overview of Birth Chart

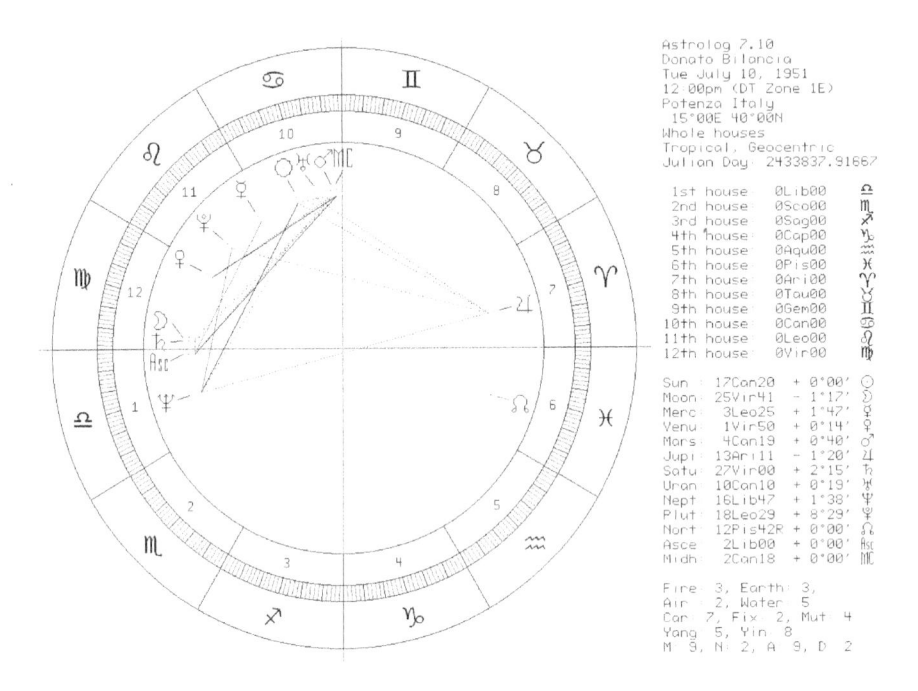

Donato Bilancia - July 10, 1951

Planets and points in the signs

Sun in Cancer- He is sensitive to the vibes around him and has a vivid recollection of memories.

Moon in Virgo– He tends to be shy, cautious, and self-critical.

Venus in Virgo- He is a perfectionist who does not tolerate faults in himself or others.

Mars in Cancer- He is easily angered when he thinks someone has slighted him.

Stellium in Cancer (Sun, Mars, Uranus)- He is hypersensitive, very emotional, and easily hurt by actions and words. Few people feel things as strongly as he does. He holds grudges and never forgives.

Stellium in Virgo (Moon, Venus, Saturn)- He is hypercritical, of both himself and others. He has a compulsive need for order and control.

Discussion:

With two stelliums in his natal chart, Donato had the overwhelming attributes of both Cancer and Virgo in his personality. The shame and pain of his childhood remained with him his entire life. The betrayal of a friend pushed him over the edge. This triggered his instincts for revenge, such as against the prostitutes who had ridiculed him.

Shared Pointers From the Natal Chart Reports

Both of these serial killers shared a stellium in Cancer. They are prone to volatile moods, have an erratic disposition, and tend to be ruled by their emotions. Both had a traumatic childhood and painful memories which triggered their killing instincts.

Chapter 5: Leo

(July 23 - August 22)
Modality - Fixed
Element - Fire

Leo Personality Traits

The positive, exemplary qualities of the Leo sign are:

- They are affectionate and outgoing.

- Leos are fiercely loyal.

- They are innovative in finding solutions to life's problems.

- Leos are generous to a fault and will share whatever they have.

- They have a dynamic approach to everything they do.

- They are warm-hearted and unselfish.

- Leos are tolerant of other viewpoints, even those radically different from their own.

Leo personalities are also prone to the following failings:

- They can become bossy and domineering.

- Normally open-minded, Leos can quickly flip and become narrow-minded.

- If they are overly conscious of their own importance, it may lead to arrogance.

- They can become adamant and opinionated, insisting that their view is the only correct way.

- Leos will use their influence to interfere in other people's affairs.

- They can become patronizing and look down on other people.

Leo is the sign of <u>fixed fire</u>. The fixed modality means Leos are persistent and will stick with a task until the bitter end. However, it can also cause them to become domineering and opinionated.

Fire in Leo is akin to a controlled burn, like a warm and radiant fireplace. As long as it is contained, the fire element is dynamic and exciting, but it comes with the risk of rapid, volatile change.

Leo Serial Killer 1: Anthony Sowell

Nickname: The Cleveland Strangler

The nickname refers to the area where he committed his atrocities.

Biography:

Anthony Edward Sowell was born on August 19, 1959, in Cleveland, Ohio, in the United States. He had six siblings and his mother, Claudia Garrison, was a single parent. His father, Thomas Sowell, was absent throughout his childhood. The family lived with Sowell's grandmother.

After his mother's sister died, Sowell's seven cousins joined the household. The two adult women regularly abused the nieces and nephews while Sowell and his siblings watched from adjacent rooms. They would strip the children naked, tie them to poles or banisters and whip them, sometimes with electrical cords.

At the age of 12, Sowell started raping his 10-year-old cousin. Other males in the household would also rape the girl on a daily basis *(Miller, 2013)*. The impact of this behavior on his personality was that rape is acceptable.

At school, Sowell had numerous social and discipline problems, and was teased and bullied by his classmates. At 18, Sowell dropped out of high school and left a pregnant girl behind to enlist in the Marine Corps.

In 1981, he married a fellow Marine, Kim Lawson, and they had at least one child together. The marriage only lasted four years. Kim Lawson died in 1998, while Sowell was serving time for rape and assault.

After his discharge from the military in 1985, Sowell began abusing drugs and alcohol. He admitted he would sometimes start drinking first thing in the morning and wouldn't stop until he blacked out.

Crime Review:

Alcohol fueled Sowell's aggression. In 1988, he was arrested for domestic violence and served eight days in jail. Other arrests between 1986-1989 included charges of disorderly conduct, DUI, and public drunkenness.

In 1989, Sowell tricked a pregnant woman into coming to his house by claiming her boyfriend was there waiting for her. When she tried to leave, he tied her up and repeatedly raped her. She managed to escape through a window after Sowell passed out drunk. She testified she thought he was going to kill her. Sowell pled guilty to the lesser charge of attempted rape and was sentenced to 15 years in prison.

After his release in 2005, Sowell was clean and sober. A psychological evaluation declared him unlikely to rape again. Instead, he became a "helper" of women who had turned to prostitution to support their crack cocaine addiction.

Sowell offered the women alcohol, friendship, and a safe place to stay on Cleveland's East Side. However, if Sowell felt betrayed by those he was trying to help, he would terrorize, attack, or rape them. Two different women testified to the police that Sowell first befriended, then later turned on them.

The niece of the mayor of Cleveland was in a relationship with Sowell until 2008. She complained about the stink in his place but thought it came from a sausage shop next door. In September 2009, Sowell abused and raped a woman whom he had invited home for drinks. She filed charges and a warrant for his arrest was issued. He was apprehended two days later.

Eleven bodies were eventually recovered in shallow graves and various spaces in and around Sowell's home. He was charged with 11 counts of murder, 74 accounts of rape, various counts of kidnapping, and abusing of corpses. After lengthy delays, he was convicted and sentenced to death.

His lawyers filed various appeals and court cases, but his sentence was finally confirmed by the Ohio Supreme Court. Anthony Sowell passed away on February 8, 2021, from a terminal illness.

Review of Birth Chart

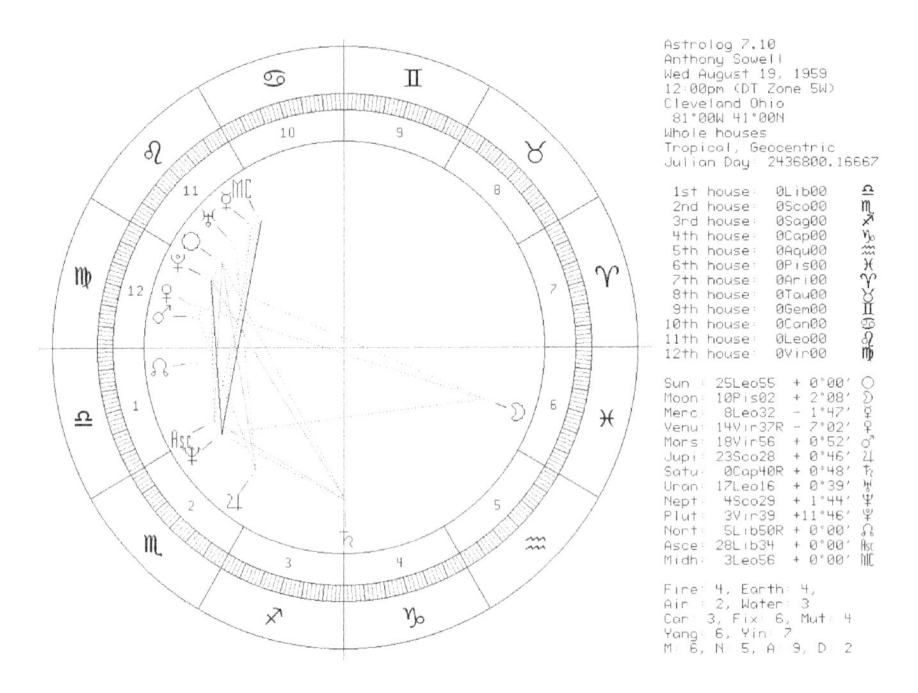

Anthony Sowell - August 19, 1959

Planets and points in the signs

Sun in Leo- He does not hesitate to use force when he thinks it is needed. He tends to be very egocentric.

Mercury in Leo- He is self-indulgent and can become aggressive if he feels he isn't getting his "due."

Venus in Virgo- He is a perfectionist who does not tolerate faults in himself or others.

Mars in Virgo- He is stubborn and demanding. He gets easily frustrated by things outside of his control.

Stellium in Leo (Sun, Mercury, Uranus)- He thrives on attention and must be in the spotlight at all times. He feels the need to take control of situations, and can become domineering and ruthless. If he doesn't get his way, he can fly into a destructive rage.

Stellium in Virgo (Venus, Mars, Pluto)- He is hypercritical, of both himself and others. He has a compulsive need for order and control.

Discussion:

Anthony Sowell's birth chart is dominated by two stelliums - one in Leo, the other in Virgo. This led to him becoming possessive, domineering, and volatile; with a "burn it all down" attitude if he didn't get what he wanted. These traits, combined with a traumatic childhood and history of rape, became the blueprint for his adult behavior.

Leo Serial Killer 2: John George Haigh

Nickname: The Acid Bath Murderer

The nickname is due to the method he used to dispose of the bodies of his victims.

Biography:

John Haigh was born in Stamford, England, on July 24, 1909, to John and Emily Haigh. The family belonged to the Plymouth Brethren, a strict Protestant sect. Because of his harsh religious upbringing, John did not have any childhood friends. He was constantly reminded that he must keep himself pure in the eyes of God, who was always watching his every move.

A choirboy at the Wakefield Cathedral, John grew up with psychotic fantasies about sacrifice and religious symbolism. As a child, he was plagued with recurring religious-themed nightmares. Some believe his claims were just a smokescreen to disguise the mind of a cold-blooded killer *(Root, 2011)*.

A talented piano player who loved classical music, John won a scholarship to Wakefield Grammar School. After graduation, he became an engineering apprentice, but left to sell insurance and advertising. He was accused of stealing and fired.

In 1934, he married Betty Hamer, but the marriage did not last. In 1936, John Haigh moved to London and set up a bogus law practice. He claimed to be a lawyer with offices all over the South of England. His scam was selling fraudulent shares, supposedly from deceased clients' estates. When a client noticed a spelling mistake on the phony letterhead, John's deception was revealed.

He was arrested for fraud and sent to jail for four years. While he was in jail, his wife gave birth to a baby girl, whom she gave up for adoption. She then divorced him. His family disowned him and ceased all contact.

Crime Review:

After his release from prison at the start of World War II, John returned to his fraudulent activities. He was arrested and sent back to prison numerous times. While in jail, he decided his arrests stemmed from the fact he left his victims alive to testify against him. He resolved to kill them from that point forward.

John became intrigued with the methods of a French killer who dissolved the corpses of his victims in acid. He was under the mistaken belief that if no body was found, no crime could be proven.

In 1943, he was released from jail. By chance, he reconnected with his old employer, William McSwan. McSwan managed properties owned by his parents, and Haigh was envious of his lifestyle. In 1944, he lured McSwan to a basement and bludgeoned him to death before dissolving his body in sulphuric acid. He informed McSwan's parents their son had fled to Scotland to avoid conscription. Haigh then moved into McSwan's house and started managing the properties.

By 1945, the war was nearing its end and McSwan's parents grew suspicious of their son's lingering absence. Under the false pretext of McSwan's surprise return, John lured the parents to the house. He killed them both, again dissolving their bodies in acid. He stole their pension checks and sold their properties before moving into a hotel in London.

Gambling consumed all of his money, so John started searching for more victims. Feigning interest in purchasing real estate, he befriended a couple who were selling a house. After winning their confidence, John lured them to his workshop and killed them with a revolver he had stolen from them. He also disposed of their bodies via acid.

His last victim was a wealthy widow who resided at the same hotel. After luring her to his workshop, he killed her and stole all her valuables. He dissolved her body, but instead of dumping it into the sewer system, he poured it into a heap of rubble. A friend of the victim reported her disappearance.

Inquiries by the police quickly established Haigh's criminal record. They found incriminating evidence related to the earlier victims. A pathologist discovered human fat, body parts, and dentures in the rubble pile. The widow's dentist identified her dentures during testimony at the trial.

Haigh pleaded insanity, citing psychotic visions caused by his strict upbringing. He also claimed to have drunk the blood of his victims. Found guilty, John Haigh was sentenced to death and hanged in August 1949.

"It is true to say that I was nurtured on Bible stories but mostly concerned with sacrifice. If by some mischance I did, or said, anything which my father regarded as improper,

he would say: 'Do not grieve the Lord by behaving so.' And if I suggested that I wanted to go somewhere, or meet somebody, he would say: 'It will not please the Lord.'"

—*John George Haigh*

Overview of Birth Chart

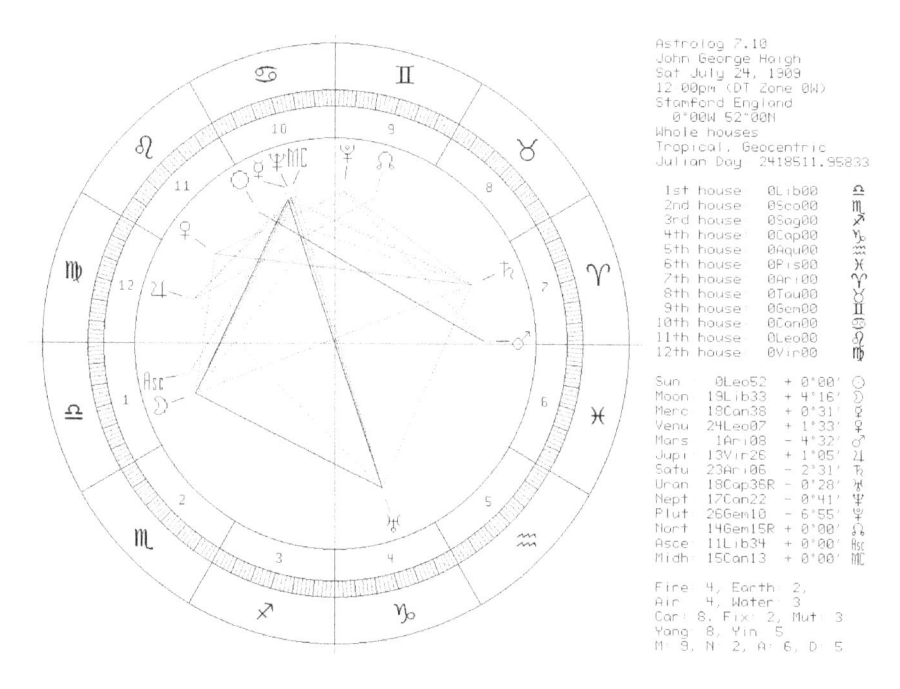

John George Haigh - July 24, 1909

Planets and points in the signs

Sun in Leo- He can be egocentric and intolerant.

Mercury in Cancer- His mind is connected with his feelings and emotions from the past.

Mars in Aries - He is self-absorbed and selfish. The desire to do things his way is very strong.

Venus in Leo - He needs constant admiration and praise.

Saturn in Aries - He feels he can govern his life by his own standards.

Neptune in Cancer - He tries to manipulate things to his advantage. He may feel chained to events from his past.

Discussion:

John Haigh displays many of the negative qualities of Leo. His planets point to an egocentric personality, where only his desires and needs are important. He craved attention and praise and was willing to do whatever it took to achieve the social status he felt he deserved. The presence of Cancer in his chart indicates that he may never have learned to let go of the trauma caused by his strict upbringing.

Shared Pointers From the Natal Chart Reports

Sowell and Haigh both share the negative traits of their sun sign, Leo. Neither hesitated to use force to satisfy their own personal needs, even if it violated accepted social norms.

Chapter 6: Virgo

(August 23 - September 22)
Modality - Mutable
Element - Earth

Virgo Personality Traits

People born under the sign of Virgo share the following strengths:

- You can depend on them to deliver on anything they have undertaken.

- Virgos are hardworking and careful in the execution of any task.

- They are intelligent, clever, and do not need constant supervision.

- Virgos are unpretentious and modest. They stay away from the limelight.

- Virgos are thorough and exacting in the performance of tasks.

- They are pragmatic and prefer not to complicate things.

- They are systematic and well-organized, both in work and everyday dealings.

- They are reserved and do not mix easily with other people.

- Virgos love patterns and routines.

The following negative attributes can be found amongst Virgos:

- Overzealous fault-finding.

- They cling to traditions and can be stubborn and resistant to change.

- They worry too much about the outcomes of things.

- Virgos can be brusque and hard towards other people.

- They can become fussy and finicky over details.

- They are sticklers for perfection and can become pedantic over it.

Virgo is a <u>mutable earth</u> sign. The earth element grounds Virgos in reality, while the mutability keeps them busy analyzing and organizing the things and people around them.

Like water, earth is considered a feminine element. Earth signs tend to be no nonsense, logical, and reliable. While earth signs are pragmatic and focused on the material world, they could become overly materialistic, even greedy and miserly. They can become so involved in their own objectives that they fail to take the feelings of others into account.

Mutable signs are the chameleons of the Zodiac - they are adaptable, flexible, and agreeable. Because they are always changing, they can also become moody and unpredictable.

Virgo Serial Killer 1: Albert DeSalvo

Nickname: The Boston Strangler

The moniker was given to a serial killer who murdered 13 women in Boston between 1962 and 1964. DeSalvo confessed to the murders but was never actually tried and convicted.

Biography:

Albert DeSalvo was born on September 3, 1931, in Chelsea, Massachusetts, in the United States. His parents were Frank and Charlotte DeSalvo. He had five siblings.

Frank DeSalvo was a violent alcoholic. In front of their children, he knocked out all of his wife's teeth and bent her fingers back until they broke. He would also bring home prostitutes and engage in sexual acts with them in front of his family.

The abuse and example set by his father were imprinted on Albert, who, at an early age, began stealing and torturing animals. In 1943, he was arrested for abuse and theft. He was sent to a reformatory. A second sojourn at the reformatory followed after an auto theft *(Frank, 2018)*.

He joined the Army and served two tours of duty, reaching the rank of sergeant. After his discharge, he seemed to settle down and married a German girl, Irmgard Beck. They had two children.

Crime Review:

Before the Boston murders began, a good-looking young man started going door-to-door in the Cambridge, Massachusetts area. He claimed to be a model scout. If the woman expressed interest, he would take her measurements while fondling her. He became known as the Measuring Man.

In 1960, Albert DeSalvo was caught for burglary and confessed to being the Measuring Man. He was sent to prison for 18 months but released early for good behavior. After his release, he began a new crime wave throughout New England as the Green Man. Dressed in green clothes, he entered more than 400 homes and raped over 300 women.

During that same time, between 1962 and 1964, 13 women were sexually assaulted and murdered in Boston:

- *June 14, 1962-* Anna Slesers, 55. Found dressed in a housecoat that had been ripped open, the cord knotted around her neck in a garish bow.

- *June 28, 1962-* Mary Mullen, 85. Found dead on the sofa in her apartment from a heart attack. Police speculate she was frightened to death.

- *June 30, 1962-* Nina Nichols, 68. Found with two stockings around her neck.

- *June 30, 1962-* Helen Blake, 65. Found on her bed, with a stocking and a bra tied around her neck.

- *Aug. 19, 1962-* Ida Irga, 75. Strangled by a pillowcase.

- *Aug. 21, 1962-* Jane Sullivan, 67. Found in her bathtub, strangled by two nylon stockings.

- *Dec. 5, 1962-* Sophie Clark, 20. Strangled by a stocking and petticoat that had been intertwined.

- *Dec. 31, 1962-* Patricia Bissette, 23. Found strangled with four articles of clothing: a knotted blouse, a nylon stocking, and two stockings tied together.

- *March 6, 1963-* Mary Brown, 69. Found strangled, beaten, and stabbed with a kitchen fork that had been left in her chest.

- *May 6, 1963-* Beverly Samans, 23. Found stabbed 16 times and strangled, with two silk scarves and a nylon stocking tied around her neck.

- *Sept. 8, 1963-* Evelyn Corbin, 58. Found on her bed with two stockings around her neck.

- *Nov. 23, 1963-* Joann Graff, 23. Found with two nylon stockings and a leotard knotted around her neck.

- *Jan. 4, 1964-* Mary Sullivan, 19. Found with a nylon stocking and two scarves around her neck.

Most of his victims were elderly. All were strangled with their own nylons or underwear, which were then neatly tied into a bow. The bodies were deliberately posed, as if for a pornographic photo. Even hardened detectives described the murders as gruesome.

In 1964, a young woman who had been assaulted by the Green Man provided the police with a description that allowed them to pinpoint Albert DeSalvo. Several other victims also positively identified him, and he was arrested for the rapes. At the time of his arrest, DeSalvo was not suspected of being involved with the Strangler murders.

DeSalvo was sent to a state hospital for psychiatric observation. There he befriended a convicted murderer, George Nassar, and admitted he was the Boston Strangler. Some people speculated that DeSalvo and Nassar worked out a deal to split the reward money if one of them confessed to the Boston murders.

DeSalvo confessed to his lawyer he was the Boston Strangler and provided details that only the perpetrator of the crime could have known. After intense questioning by the police, they were convinced that they had finally caught the Boston Strangler. No physical evidence was found to link DeSalvo to the murders, and he was never formally charged. Instead, he was sentenced to life in prison for the Green Man rapes.

In February 1967, DeSalvo and two fellow inmates escaped from Bridgewater State Hospital, triggering a full-scale manhunt. Three days later, he voluntarily turned himself in.

DeSalvo was then transferred to Walpole maximum security prison, where he recanted his Boston Strangler confession. A former prison psychologist who analyzed both men believes it was George Nassar, not DeSalvo, who actually committed the Strangler murders. He claims DeSalvo only confessed because he wanted the notoriety; he hoped the case would make him world-famous.

In 1973, DeSalvo was killed in his cell by a fellow inmate.

In 2013, the Boston Police uncovered DNA evidence from the Boston Strangler's final victim. When a DNA sample donated by DeSalvo's nephew proved to be a reasonable match, DeSalvo's body was exhumed and tested. The evidence proved that DeSalvo was indeed the killer, thus linking him to at least one victim of the Boston Strangler.

> *"People everywhere, are still in doubt. The Strangler, in prison, or roaming about?"* - Albert DeSalvo

Overview of Birth Chart

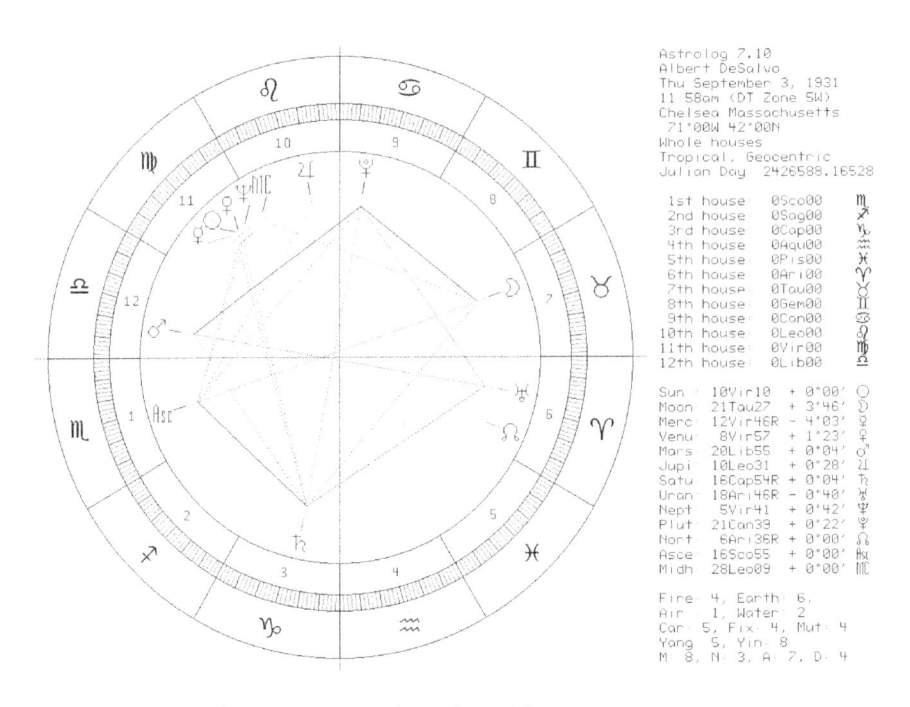

```
Astrolog 7.10
Albert DeSalvo
Thu September 3, 1931
11:58am (DT Zone 5W)
Chelsea Massachusetts
71°00W 42°00N
Whole houses
Tropical, Geocentric
Julian Day: 2426588.16528

1st house    0Sco00    ♏
2nd house    0Sag00    ♐
3rd house    0Cap00    ♑
4th house    0Aqu00    ♒
5th house    0Pis00    ♓
6th house    0Ari00    ♈
7th house    0Tau00    ♉
8th house    0Gem00    ♊
9th house    0Can00    ♋
10th house   0Leo00    ♌
11th house   0Vir00    ♍
12th house   0Lib00    ♎

Sun   10Vir10  + 0°00'  ☉
Moon  21Tau27  + 3°46'  ☽
Merc  12Vir46R - 4°03'  ☿
Venu   8Vir57  + 1°23'  ♀
Mars  20Lib55  + 0°04'  ♂
Jupi  10Leo31  + 0°28'  ♃
Satu  16Cap54R + 0°04'  ♄
Uran  18Ari46R - 0°40'  ♅
Nept   5Vir41  + 0°42'  ♆
Plut  21Can39  + 0°22'  ♇
Nort   6Ari36R + 0°00'  ☊
Asce  16Sco55  + 0°00'  Asc
Midh  28Leo09  + 0°00'  MC

Fire: 4, Earth: 6,
Air:  1, Water: 2
Car: 5, Fix: 4, Mut: 4
Yang: 5, Yin: 8
M: 8, N: 3, A: 7, D: 4
```

<u>Albert DeSalvo - September 3, 1931</u>

Planets and points in the signs

Scorpio rising- This is a powerful rising sign, and his higher and lower natures are in conflict. He experiences everything intensely. He is secretive and withdrawn, unable to control his passions.

Sun in Virgo- He loves patterns and routines. He may be depressed and self-centered. He can become touchy if someone criticizes him.

Moon in Taurus- He tends to overindulge in sensual pleasures.

Mercury in Virgo- He has high expectations of himself and others. He can become harsh and judgmental if his expectations aren't met.

Jupiter in Leo - Happiest in the spotlight, he needs to be the center of attention.

Leo in Midheaven - The Midheaven indicates his legacy; his lasting achievement in life. With Leo in this position, he is prone to drama, scandal, and general extravagance.

Stellium in Virgo (Sun, Mercury, Venus, Neptune)- He is hypercritical of both himself and others. He has a compulsive need for order and control. His focus is on getting everything perfect, down to the most minute detail.

Planets and points in the houses

Leo in the 10th house- He is proud of his accomplishments and wants to be recognized for his work.

Stellium in the 11th house- He may feel unloved and unlovable. He has few family ties. He expects a lot from others and becomes disillusioned when they fail to deliver.

Discussion:

With a Virgo stellium in his 11th house, Albert DeSalvo was born with many attributes that could have made him an effective team leader. Instead, these positive characteristics were warped and twisted by an abusive childhood.

As a Scorpio rising, he needed to experience everything intensely and had no control over his baser passions. Leo in his Midheaven and 10th house drove him to be desperate for fame. He took credit for the killings, even if he may not have been responsible for all of them.

Virgo Serial Killer 2: Henry Lee Lucas

Nickname: The Confession Killer

Lucas received the nickname after confessing to killing more than 3,000 people. The confessions were later retracted and most were shown to be a hoax.

Biography:

Henry Lee Lucas was born on August 23, 1936, in a one-room log cabin in Blacksburg, Virginia, in the United States. His parents, Anderson and Viola Lucas, were both alcoholics. He was the youngest of nine children.

His father, Anderson "No Legs" Lucas, lost his legs in a railroad accident. He started bootlegging illegal alcohol to make a living. His mother prostituted herself in their backwoods community to earn money.

A harsh and abusive person, Viola ruled their household with an iron fist. She despised her youngest son and allowed her boyfriend, "Uncle Bernie," to beat him regularly. When Henry was 8 years old, Viola hit him on the head with a wooden plank so hard, he spent three days in a coma. She made Henry watch her having sex with clients, hoping to turn him into a sex worker.

When Lucas started attending school, his mother forced him to wear girls' clothing to class. This only stopped when his teachers obtained a court order. At the age of 10, Lucas lost an eye when it became infected after a fight with one of his brothers (*Henderson, 1998*).

In 1949, Lucas' father passed out in a blizzard and froze to death. Shortly thereafter, Lucas dropped out of school in the sixth grade. He ran away from home and started drifting across Virginia.

Lucas' sexual deviancy grew increasingly pronounced as a teenager. His older half-brother and "Uncle Bernie" introduced him to bestiality and animal torture.

Crime Review:

Henry later confessed that in 1951, he killed a 17-year-old girl who refused to have sex with him, but this has not been substantiated. In 1954, Lucas was jailed for four years for various burglaries.

After his release in 1959, he moved to Michigan to stay with his half-sister. His mother, Viola, came to visit for Christmas. In January 1960, they got into a fight which escalated out of control. According to Henry, Viola hit him over the head with a broom handle. He stabbed her in the neck and fled the scene. She died of a heart attack before medical help could arrive.

Even though Lucas claimed self-defense, he was sentenced to 40 years in prison for his mother's murder. He was released in 1970 due to overcrowding in the jails.

In 1971, he was sentenced to 5 years for attempted kidnapping. Upon his release, he moved to Pennsylvania and married Betty Crawford, the widow of a cousin. He left her after she accused him of molesting her two daughters.

In 1976, Lucas became friends with Ottis Toole, a fellow sexual deviant from Jacksonville, Florida. Lucas moved into Toole's home where he fell in love with his 10-year-old niece, Frieda "Becky" Powell.

Between 1979 to 1981, Lucas and Toole worked together at a roofing company. Lucas later claimed to have murdered hundreds of victims during that time; some he killed on his own, others he butchered with Toole on the orders of a satanic, cannibalistic cult called "The Hands of Death."

Lucas convinced Becky, now 15, to run away with him. They lived on the road, traveling to California, where they found employment in caring for 82-year-old Kate Rich. They were caught stealing from Kate Rich and kicked out.

In 1982, Becky grew homesick and demanded to return to Florida. On the way, Lucas killed her in an argument. Three weeks later, Kate Rich went missing and Lucas was the prime suspect. He was arrested.

After four days in jail, Lucas pleaded guilty to the two murders and went on to claim to have committed over a hundred additional murders. Over the following year and a half, he confessed to hundreds of murders. A dedicated "Lucas Task Force" was established. For his assistance, authorities flew Lucas across states, where he stayed in motels and was served steaks and milkshakes.

213 homicide cases were closed based on Lucas' confessions, but his claims became increasingly outlandish. Suspicious detectives began to make up crimes to see if Lucas would confess. He did. When it came to light that Lucas had been given access to confidential case files on his supposed crimes, the task force was discredited. Most of Lucas' confessions were thrown out.

Opinions still differ on the number of murders for which Lucas was actually responsible. He was ultimately convicted of 11 killings, but only 3 were proven. He died in 2001 from heart problems.

Overview of Birth Chart

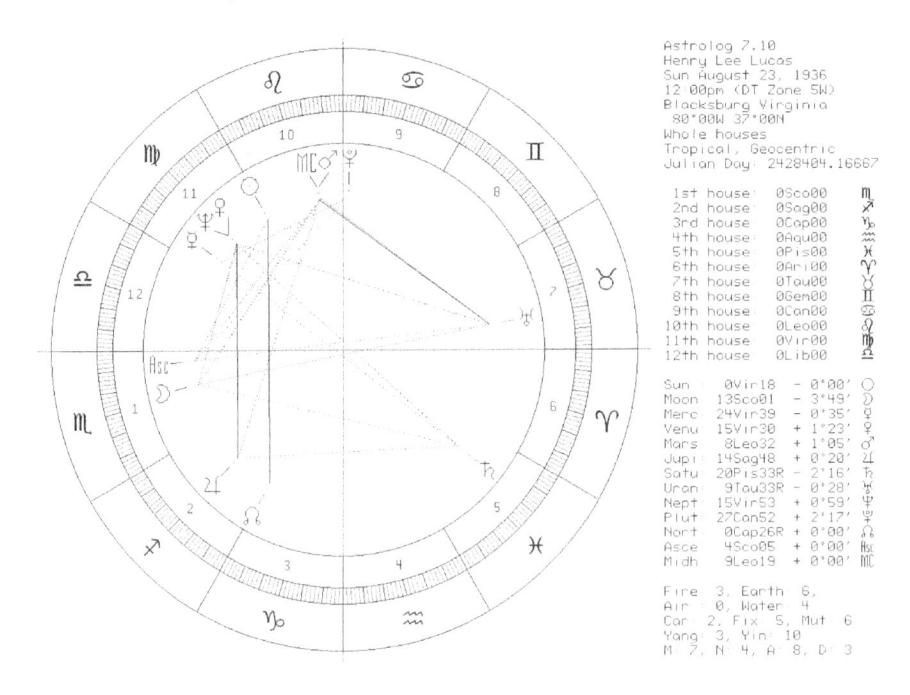

Henry Lee Lucas - August 23, 1936

Planets and points in the signs

Sun in Virgo- He appreciates luxurious things, and may be tempted and manipulated with bribes.

Moon in Scorpio- He loves with passion and hates with passion. Everything is done emotionally, with intensity. His

98

mother was very controlling. He has a habit of holding onto wrongs that have been done in the past, not forgiving nor forgetting, and he is keeping these feelings to himself.

Mercury in Virgo- He has high expectations of himself and others. He can become harsh and judgmental if these expectations aren't met.

Mars in Leo- He loves gambling and taking risks. He tends to be boastful.

Stellium in Virgo (Sun, Mercury, Venus, Neptune)- He is quick to help others and offer his services and expertise. He has a compulsive need for order and control. His focus is on getting everything perfect, down to the most minute detail. He can become materialistic and greedy.

Discussion:

Everything Henry Lucas did seems to have been shaped and influenced by his mother, leading to him ultimately killing her. With a Virgo stellium, Lucas was eager to help the police with their other investigations, and if it meant certain perks for him, even better. The murders were influenced by the deep feelings and passions of his Scorpio rising. His Mars in Leo felt the need to brag about his exploits, which may be the basis for his false confessions.

Shared Pointers From the Natal Chart Reports

Both subjects share Scorpio rising and a Virgo stellium. Scorpio rising in Virgo is a very powerful sign and leads to strong emotional reactions. Given the influence from the abuse by their parents, their emotions manifest in all the negative ways. Prominent Leo placements in both charts compelled them to seek fame and attention for their crimes.

Chapter 7: Libra

(September 23 - October 22)
Modality - Cardinal
Element - Air

Libra Personality Traits

Libra people display the following positive attributes:

- Their manners are sophisticated and they are polite in any company.

- Libras are romantic, passionate, and do not like to be alone.

- They are peaceful and tend to avoid conflict.

- They see the world and situations through rose-colored glasses and may have unrealistic expectations.

- They are even-tempered and not easily ruffled.

- Libras are tactful, well-mannered, and possess the ability to deal smoothly with difficult situations.

- Social intercourse is important to Libras and they enjoy the company of other people.

- Charisma is a key attribute of all Libras; they love to get along with everyone.

Libras have their shortcomings as well:

- They find it difficult to choose, with trouble deciding between different alternatives.

- Since Libras change to fit in with people and their surroundings, it becomes difficult to pinpoint their actual personality.

- They can be impressionable and easily influenced by the opinions of others.

- Libras like to flirt but set a high value on stable relationships.

- They can be easily misled by false presentations.

- Libras love the finer things in life and can be self-indulgent.

Libra is the sign of <u>cardinal</u> <u>air</u>. The role of cardinal signs is to push forward and initiate. They are the first to start a project, but they generally lack the focus to see things through to completion. Libras are good at telling others what to do, but often procrastinate over deciding for themselves. They can also be pessimistic.

The air of Libra is like breath, gently flowing in and out. The Air element represents activities such as talking, thinking, comprehending, learning, and sharing information. Individuals with prominent air in their charts can be elusive and hard to read. They are also prone to being unpredictable, detached, insensitive, and impractical.

Libra Serial Killer 1: Carlton Gary

Nickname: The Stocking Strangler

His nickname was derived from the method used to kill his victims.

Biography:

Carlton Gary was born on September 24, 1950, in Columbus. Georgia, in the United States. The names of his parents are not known, but his father was a construction worker who rejected his son and any responsibility for him. His mother was poor, and he spent much of his childhood in a state of near starvation.

They moved around constantly as his mother was either looking for or working on short temporary jobs. Since his mother could not always take him along to work, his aunt and great aunt often took care of him. Both worked as servants for rich, elderly ladies.

During the 1950s and 60s, segregation was still very much a way of life in the Southern United States. White employers could abuse and misuse their African American servants without fear of repercussion. Seeing his mother and aunts subjected to ill treatment may have sowed the seeds for Gary's eventual killing spree, since he specifically targeted elderly white women *(Rose, 2011)*.

Gary suffered a serious head due to a playground accident at school. As a teenager, he became a heavy user of drugs and alcohol. He logged his first arrest in 1966. Between the ages of 14 and 18, his rap sheet included charges of robbery, arson, and assault.

While still in his teens, he married Sheila Gary, and they had two children together. The marriage did not last. It is not recorded what became of his wife and children.

Crime Review:

In 1970, Gary moved to Albany in New York, where he continued with his criminal activities. Soon after he arrived in Albany, an elderly lady, Marion Brewer, was attacked and robbed in her hotel room. Suspicion was cast on Gary, but he was never convicted of the crime.

Two months later, in July 1970, Gary strangled 85-year-old Nellie Farmer. After he attempted to assault a third elderly woman, Gary was arrested. His fingerprints matched prints found at the Farmer murder scene. He admitted to robbing her but blamed the actual murder on an accomplice, John Mitchell. Gary was convicted of burglary, receiving stolen property, and possession of drugs.

After being paroled in 1975, he moved to Syracuse, New York, where he raped and strangled two elderly ladies within four days of each other. One was killed, but the other survived. The survivor could not positively identify her attacker, because it was too dark for her to see his face.

Gary was never charged for these murders; instead, he found himself back in prison on a parole violation. In August 1977,

Gary escaped from the low-security facility by sawing through the bars of his cell.

He made his way back to Columbus, Georgia, where he began the killing spree that earned him the nickname, "The Stocking Strangler."

- *September 16, 1977-* Ferne Jackson, 60. Raped and strangled with a silk stocking.

- *September 25, 1977-* Jean Dimenstein, 71. Raped and strangled with a silk stocking.

- *October 21, 1977-* Florence Scheible, 89. Raped and strangled with a silk stocking.

- *October 25, 1977-* Martha Thurmond, 69. Raped and strangled with a silk stocking.

- *December 28, 1977-* Kathleen Woodruff, 74. Raped and strangled with no silk stocking left on the scene.

- *February 12, 1978-* Attacked Ruth Schwob but fled after she triggered an alarm.

- *February 12, 1978-* Mildred Boron, 78. Raped and strangled with a silk stocking. This was just two blocks away from Ruth Schwob.

- *April 20, 1978-* Janet Cofer, 61. Raped and strangled with a silk stocking.

By early March, police knew they were searching for a black man. Since the Strangler's victims had been white, there was a growing threat of racial violence.

To complicate matters, another killer — who called himself "Chairman of the Forces of Evil" — sent messages to the police threatening to kill a black woman for each of the Strangler's white victims until he was swiftly apprehended.

This second killer, a black man named William Henry Hance, was arrested on April 4, 1978. Hance had been trying to cover up three murders of his own by pinning the blame on white vigilantes. Police suspected Hance might be the Strangler, but Cofer's death convinced them the actual killer was still at large.

In December 1978, following a string of robberies in South Carolina, Gary was arrested and sentenced to 21 years for armed robbery. He escaped from custody a second time and lived as a fugitive for 14 months before he was finally captured in Albany, Georgia.

New evidence had emerged while Gary was in hiding. His fingerprints were found at four of the Strangler crime scenes. Gary was arrested, convicted, and received a death sentence in August 1986.

There are many controversies surrounding the case, ranging from an unsigned and undated confession, fingerprint matching performed years after the trial, and other inconsistencies in the preparation and handling of evidence.

In 2007, Gary was linked through a DNA test to the murder of Marion Fisher in 1975. After numerous appeals and other legal procedures, he was finally executed on March 15, 2018.

Overview of Birth Chart

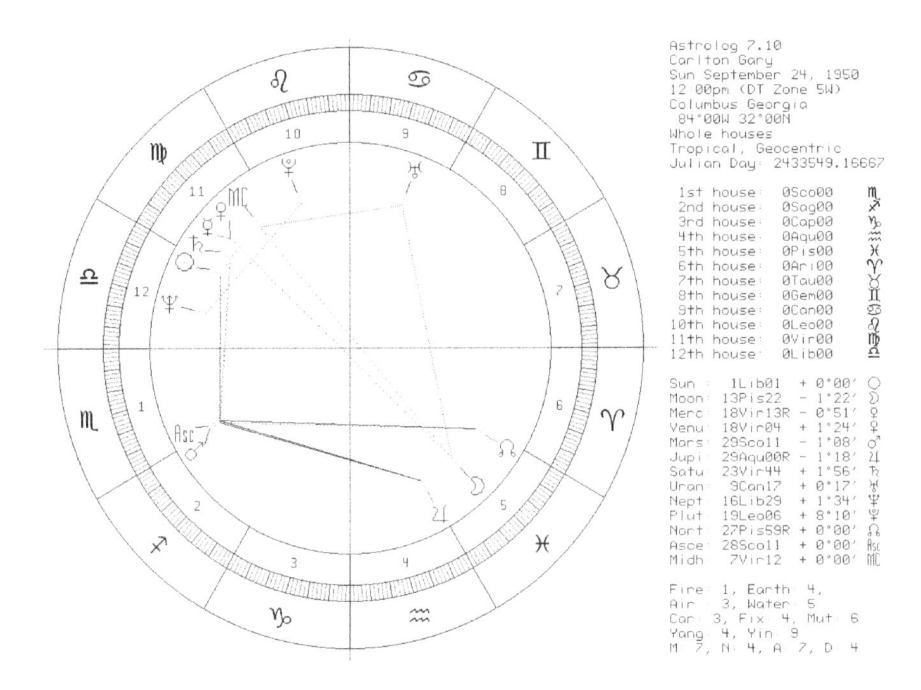

Carlton Gary - September 24, 1950

Planets and points in the signs

Sun in Libra- He feels the need to take action around principles of fairness, justice, and equality.

Moon in Pisces- He is very sensitive and emotional. The women in his life, especially his mother, had a great impression on him as a child.

Venus in Virgo- He is a perfectionist who does not tolerate faults in himself or others.

Mars in Scorpio- His likes and dislikes are strong and intense, never casual or superficial. He is known for his persistence and willful obsession. Once he has decided on a course of action, he is unstoppable. His emotional actions tend to be extreme.

Saturn in Virgo- He is very methodical. His compulsive habits may appear neurotic to outside observers. He is prone to obsessive-compulsive disorders.

Stellium in Virgo (Mercury, Venus, Saturn)- He has a compulsive need for order and control. He feels used and abused by the system, and is compelled to rise up against the system to regain control.

Discussion:

Carlton Gary is a product of his times and childhood. The discrimination he and his family faced would have triggered his Libra need for balance and fairness. His Scorpio Mars pushed him to take extreme action through his Virgo stellium.

Virgo is the sign associated with slavery. When coupled with Saturn, it indicates a breaking free from the shackles and reclaiming your authority.

The wrongdoings Gary experienced as a child were directly channeled into negative extremes as predicted by his horoscope.

Libra Serial Killer 2: Angelo Anthony Buono Jr.

Nickname: The Hillside Strangler

The name was popularized by the media as a name for the murders committed by Angelo Buono and his cousin Kenneth Bianchi during 1977 and 1978.

Biography:

Anthony Buono was born on October 5, 1934, in Rochester, New York *(Bardsley, 2006)*. His parents were Angelo and Jenny Buono, first generation Italian-Americans who emigrated to the United States from San Buono, Italy. He had one sister.

His parents divorced in 1939 and Angelo moved to Glendale, California, with his mother and sister. His mother supported the family by working in a shoe factory. Angelo was raised Catholic, but his religion had little impact on him.

At an early age, Buono started showing indications of psychiatric problems. He loathed women and verbally abused his mother. In addition to misogyny, he had a sadistic streak that intensified as he grew older.

Buono displayed a high interest in sex at a young age. As a fourteen-year-old, he would brag to his schoolmates about raping and sodomizing girls. His hero and role model was the notorious rapist, Caryl Chessman. Chessman would impersonate a police officer to lure women into his car and sexually assault them.

In 1955, Buono married his high-school sweetheart, 17-year-old Geraldine Vinal, whom he had impregnated. He left her after less than a week. Later he divorced her and refused to pay child support.

In 1957, he married Mary Castillo. They had five children together, but in 1964, this marriage also ended in divorce. Castillo claimed Buono was physically and sexually abusive; he would beat and kick her in front of their children.

When Buono refused to pay child support, Castillo was forced to go on welfare. She tried to reconcile with him to support her children, but after he handcuffed and threatened her at gunpoint, she realized reconciliation was impossible. In 2007, Mary Castillo was murdered by her own grandson who then committed suicide.

For his third wife, Buono married a single mother named Nannette Campino. They had two children. Buono also physically abused Campino, but she stayed with him because he threatened to kill her if she tried to leave. In 1971, Campino decided it was worth the risk when she learned Buono had raped her 14-year-old daughter. She and her children fled the state to escape from him.

Despite Buono's abusive behavior, women found his macho Italian image appealing. A year later, he married another woman named Deborah Taylor, but they didn't live together.

Buono's troubles with the law started in his teenage years, when he was sent to reform school for grand theft auto. By the mid-1970s, he had acquired a long criminal history ranging from failure to pay child support, to theft, rape, and assault.

Crime Review:

Angelo Buono had a small car upholstery shop attached to his house, which supplied the private seclusion for him to engage in his sexual and sadistic acts with local girls.

In 1975 his adopted cousin, Kenneth Bianchi, moved in with him. Buono and Bianchi started a new business as brothel-keepers. Bianchi would lure young girls to Buono's house, where they were kept in captivity and forced into prostitution. After their two girls escaped, they needed more prostitutes to keep the business going.

Posing as undercover police officers with fake police badges, the pair attempted to abduct a girl. But when they learned she was Catherine Lorre, daughter of famed Hungarian actor Peter Lorre, they let her go.

Instead, they decided to purchase a list of prostitutes. The list turned out to be bogus. Realizing they'd been conned, they wanted revenge but could only find the seller's friend, a prostitute named Yolanda Washington. On October 16, 1977, Buono and Bianchi raped and killed Washington.

They continued to impersonate police officers, cruising around Los Angeles to pick up girls. They would order the women into their car, then take them to the shop where they would be tortured, abused, raped, and killed.

Although strangulation was their primary modus operandi, they experimented with other methods of killing, including gas asphyxiation, lethal injection, and electric shock. The bodies were disposed of outdoors, often in hilly areas, hence the nickname, "The Hillside Strangler."

Between October 1977 and February 1978 they murdered a total of ten women:

- *October 17, 1977*– Cathedral City. Yolanda Washington, 19. Beaten, raped, strangled.

- *October 31, 1977*– La Crescenta. Montrose: Judith Ann Miller, 15. Raped, sodomized, strangled.

- *November 5, 1977*– Glendale. Elissa Teresa Kastin, 21. Beaten, raped, and strangled.

- *November 13, 1977*- Highland Park. Dolores Cepeda, 14. Raped and strangled.

- *November 13, 1977*- Highland Park. Sonja Johnson, 12. Raped and strangled.

- *November 20, 1977*- Highland Park. Kristin Weckler, 20. Sexually assaulted, tortured with Windex injections, and fatally asphyxiated with gas from an oven.

- *November 23, 1977*- Los Angeles. Jane Evelyn King, 28. Sodomized and strangled.

- *November 28, 1977*- Glassell Park. Lauren Rae Wagner, 18. Tortured by electrocution and fatally strangled.

- *December 9, 1977*- Echo Park. Kimberly Diane Martin, 17. strangled.

- *February 16, 1978-* La Cañada Flintridge. Cindy Lee Hudspeth, 20. Sexually violated and fatally strangled.

Los Angeles police suspected the "Strangler" was actually two men working together. An unusual twist to their investigation was a psychic from Berlin. She wrote in German what they should look for:

Two Italians. Brothers. Aged about thirty-five.

Detectives questioned Bianchi about one of the Strangler murders that may have taken place in his apartment building. The detectives did not consider him a suspect. In fact, they allowed him to take part in LAPD's ride-along program, which let civilians go along in patrol cars while the police looked for the killers. When Buono learned Bianchi was talking to the police, he threatened to kill him if he didn't get out of town.

Bianchi moved to Washington to be with his girlfriend, but he was, by now, so used to his murderous lifestyle that he killed Karen Mandic and Diane Wilder in January 1979. He was immediately suspected of the crimes and interrogated. Enough evidence was found at Bianchi's home to convict him of the killings.

The similarities between the Washington murders and the Hillside Strangler were enough to contact the Los Angeles police who questioned Bianchi. For a plea bargain to avoid the death sentence, Bianchi agreed to testify against Buono.

The legal case against Buono was based largely upon Bianchi's testimony, but he proved to be an unreliable witness. Bianchi claimed, among other things, to have amnesia and multiple personalities.

Buono's trial would become the longest in American legal history, lasting from November 1981 until November 1983. Eventually, Angelo Buono was sentenced to life in prison. He died in 2002 from a heart attack.

Overview of Birth Chart

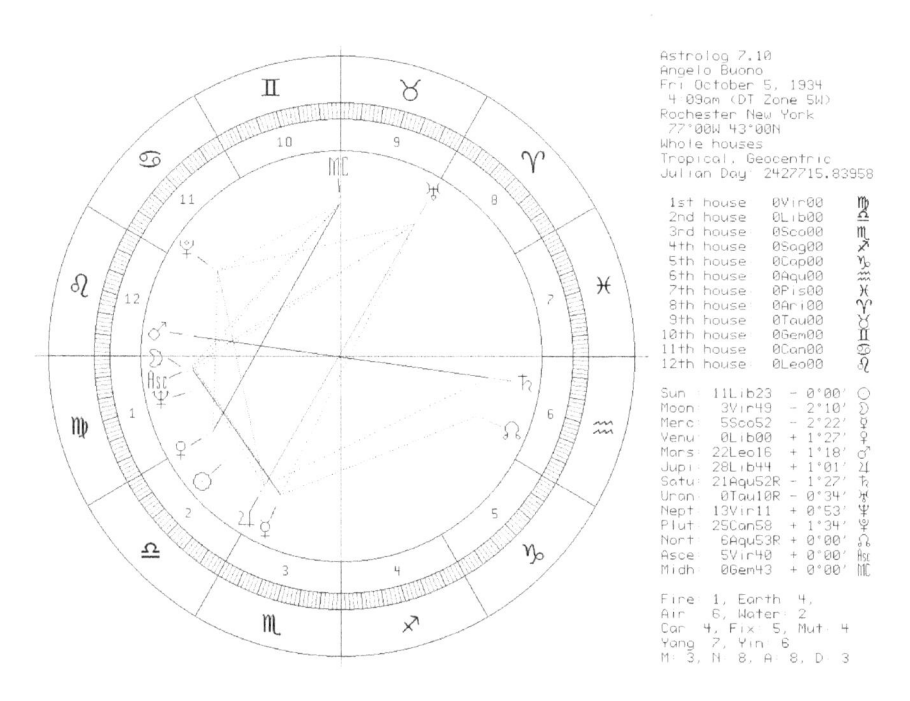

Angelo Buono - October 5, 1934

Planets and points in the signs

Sun in Libra- He is narcissistic and self-indulgent. He also holds grudges and seeks revenge on those he feels have wronged him.

Mars in Leo- He is competitive and likes to be "number one." He is proud, aggressive, confident, dramatic, and enthusiastic.

Libra Stellium (Sun, Venus, Jupiter)- He is prone to emotional meltdowns and may lash out and attack those close to him. He has a superiority complex and looks down on others.

Planets and points in the houses

Stellium in the 2nd house- He has a strong need to possess things (and by extension, people).

Mars in the 12th house- He suppresses his emotions and has a secretive nature. He has unresolved feelings of rage from his childhood that he projects onto others. If he turns to a life a crime, one of his accomplices will probably snitch.

Discussion:

Angelo Buono's chart is dominated by a Libra stellium in his 2nd house of possessions. One interesting side-effect of stelliums is that, because of the imbalance of energy, they may channel excess energy into the house directly opposite them. In Buono's case, this falls in his 8th house of sex and death. Mars in his 12th house of false friends and hidden enemies became apparent when his cousin testified against him to the police.

Shared Pointers From the Natal Chart Reports

Both subjects share a Sun in Libra. For Carlton Gary, seems to have manifested as a need to balance the injustices in society. For Angelo Buono, it twisted into a hateful superiority complex where he no longer saw humans as people but as possessions.

Chapter 8: Scorpio

(October 23 - November 21)
Modality - Fixed
Element - Water

Scorpio Personality Traits

Scorpios share the following strengths:

- They can be strong-willed and assertive.
- Scorpios easily exert influence over their surroundings and other people.
- They are charismatic and engaging.
- Scorpios handle relationships with passion and intensity.
- Scorpios are persistent; once they find something they want, they will pursue it without stopping.
- Scorpios rely on intuition to guide them.
- They form strong emotional bonds.
- Due to their intense emotions, Scorpios are exciting, but also have a secretive side that can be dangerous.

Scorpios are subject to the following shortcomings:

- Strong feelings and attachments may cause intense bouts of jealousy.
- They can become controlling and fixated on relationships and situations.
- Scorpios have a clear idea of their mission and purpose; anything that hinders them will be resented and remembered for later retaliation.

- Scorpios can be overpowering; they believe they can meet any challenge and subdue it with their sharp intellect.

- They can be quite stubborn; they know what they want and do not need to accommodate anyone else.

- Scorpios are secretive and do not share their objectives with outsiders.

Scorpio is the sign of fixed water. Scorpio is often mistaken for a fire sign because of their passionate nature and forceful personalities. That is a dangerous mistake. The water of Scorpio is akin to the ocean, teeming with hidden life deep below the surface. Scorpio's emotions are extreme, dark, and mysterious. They represent the unknown, secretive aspects of the Zodiac.

Scorpio Serial Killer 1: Charles Manson

Nickname: None

Charles Manson named his cult followers The Family and required them all to adopt different names.

Biography:

Charles Manson was born on November 12, 1934, in Cincinnati, Ohio, in the United States, as "no name Maddox." His parents were Colonel Walker Henderson Scott Sr. and 16-year-old Kathleen Maddox. Walker was a mill worker and con artist; he convinced Maddox he was an Army officer, when Colonel was, in fact, his first name. When Walker learned of Maddox's pregnancy, he left town on "military business" and never returned. It's unlikely Charles ever met his birth father.

Before the baby was born, Kathleen married William Manson, a laborer at a dry cleaning business. She later changed her son's name to Charles Manson *(Guinn, 2014)*. Kathleen Maddox and her brother, Luther, would go on drinking sprees, leaving Charles with his stepfather. William filed for divorce in 1937.

In 1939, Kathleen was arrested with her brother and sentenced to 5 years in jail for assault and robbery. Charles was placed with an uncle and aunt until his mother was released on parole in 1942.

Charles Manson started getting into trouble at an early age. At the age of nine, he set his school on fire. In 1947, at 13, Manson was caught for truancy and petty theft and sent to a Catholic reform school for male delinquents in Indiana. The priests were very strict; punishment for even the tiniest infraction included beatings with a wooden paddle or a leather strap.

Manson ran away from school and made his way back home, sleeping in the woods, under bridges, and wherever else he could find shelter. He spent Christmas with his mother, who then returned him to the reformatory. Ten months later, he ran away again, this time heading for Indianapolis.

In 1948, he committed his first known crime - he robbed a grocery store for money and food.

Crime Review:

Manson got a job as a Western Union message boy, supplementing his income with petty theft. When he was caught in 1949, the judge sentenced him to Boys Town, a juvenile detention facility in Omaha, Nebraska. After four days, he ran away with a fellow student named Blackie Nielson. They stole a car and gun and committed robberies on their way to Nielson's uncle. The uncle was a professional thief and took the boys in as apprentices.

Two weeks later, Mason was caught robbing a store and sent to the Indiana Boys School, a strict reform school. Here he was raped and assaulted by other inmates, under the encouragement of the staff. He ran away eighteen times.

In 1951, Manson finally managed to escape with two other boys. They stole a car and attempted to drive to California.

They made it as far as Utah, robbing filling stations along the way, until they were caught and sent to the National Training School for Boys in Washington, DC. Manson's case worker determined he was illiterate and aggressively antisocial.

In 1951, Manson was transferred to a minimum-security institution. After sodomizing another boy at knife-point, he was assigned to the Federal Reformatory in Virginia, where he committed a series of serious offenses. He was then sentenced to a maximum security reformatory in Ohio, where he was expected to stay until he turned 21.

Manson was released for good behavior in 1954. He married a waitress and stole a car to drive to Los Angeles. For crossing state lines in a stolen vehicle, Manson was sentenced to five years' probation; but failed to appear at a hearing and was imprisoned for three years. His wife gave birth while he was in prison, then divorced him and moved in with another man. In 1958, he was paroled.

In 1959, Manson was convicted of trying to cash a forged treasury check and received a 10-year suspended sentence. He was arrested in Texas for running a multi-state prostitution ring. For violating the terms of his probation, Mason was sent to federal prison in Washington state to serve out his 10-year sentence. By the time he was released in 1967, Manson had spent more than half his life incarcerated.

During the period from 1957 to 1967, Charles Manson began exploring ways to achieve fame in Hollywood. He learned guitar, studied the popular bands of the era, developed ambitions to be a singer and songwriter, and sought connections at film studios. He studied religion and social engineering as tools of manipulation and control, especially L. Ron Hubbard's Church of Scientology. From brothel-keepers and pimps he met in prison, Manson mastered the tactics of bringing women completely under his control.

Upon his release in March 1967, Manson moved to San Francisco, the epicenter of the burgeoning Hippie movement. Manson traveled throughout California as a religious figure and spiritual guru, manipulating and recruiting new followers into the cult he called "The Family. He brainwashed his followers into blindly surrendering their identities and supporting him through theft and petty crime.

In late 1967, Manson moved The Family to Los Angeles to pursue his dream of becoming a star. He started using the contacts he had made in prison. Universal Studios granted him a recording session, but he was a disaster. His most valuable connection was Dennis Wilson of the Beach Boys. Throughout 1968, Wilson allowed The Family to live in his house and lent them money to produce a record in exchange for sexual favors from female cult members.

Wilson introduced Manson to record producer, Terry Melcher, and they became friends. The Beach Boys even recorded one of Manson's songs. However, the relationship between Manson and Wilson soured after the song was released. When Manson discovered his lyrics had been changed and he was denied songwriter credit, he threatened to kill Wilson. These violent threats, along with Manson's lack of talent, bigotry, and racism, caused Melcher to end their friendship.

By the middle of 1969, Manson's Hollywood dreams had evaporated and he transformed The Family into a doomsday cult. He believed an apocalyptic race war - which he dubbed "Helter Skelter" after a Beatles song - was imminent and The Family would emerge as the new leaders.

In August 1969, Charles Manson instructed his followers to start Helter Skelter by committing racially motivated murders. On August 8th and 9th, Actress Sharon Tate and four others were killed in the house where Melcher used to stay. On August 10th, they murdered Leno and Rosemary LaBianca.

At Tate Murder trial, the four defendants were sentenced to death, but all were later commuted to life sentences. Altogether, The Family were linked to at least six murders.

In the years following the Tate Murders, members of The Family continued to perpetrate various crimes, the last of which was an attempted assassination of President Gerald Ford in 1975.

Charles Manson died from cancer on November 19, 2017. As for other members of the Family, some are still in prison.

"You've got to accept yourself as God. You've got to realize you're just the devil just as much as you're God, that you're everything and you're nothing at all."

- Charles Manson

Overview of Birth Chart

Planets and points in the signs

Sun in Scorpio- Because his unconscious mind is more in control than his conscious mind, he loses all sense of judgment under criticism. He tends to do things to extremes,

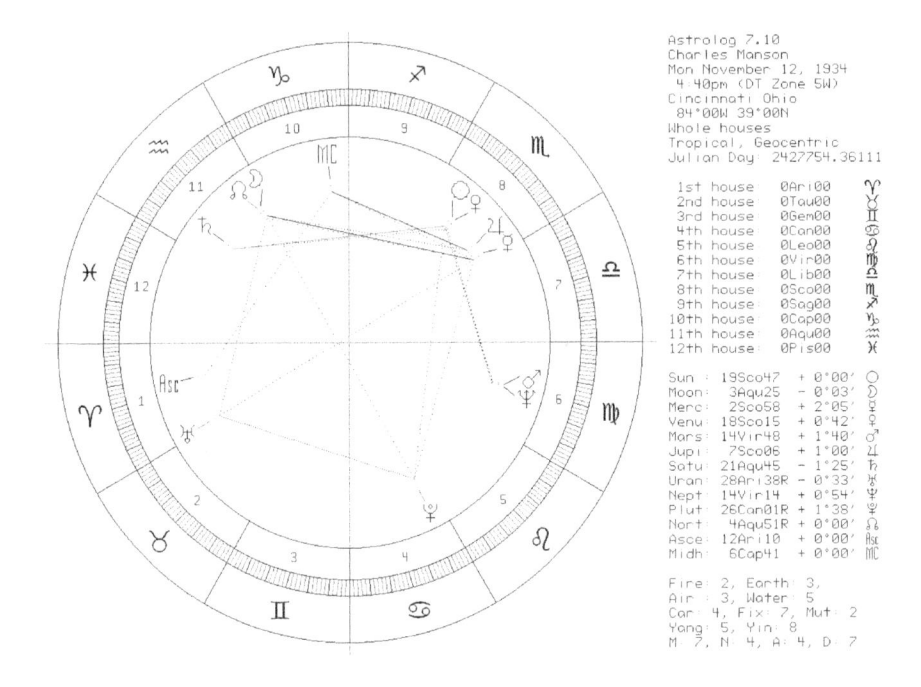

Charles Manson - November 12, 1934

either all or nothing. There are powerful emotions and desires at work within him, underneath the surface.

Moon in Aquarius- He feels above the trivial, day-to-day aspects of life, and prefers to focus on bigger, world-changing matters. He mays become so fixated on his grand vision that he overlooks the feelings of others.

Mercury in Scorpio- He is outspoken, stubborn, and quick to get into arguments.

Venus in Scorpio- He demands complete loyalty from those in his circle. He feels the need to control and possess those around him.

Jupiter in Scorpio- He has a magnetic personality; people are attracted to his mysterious and alluring nature. He refuses to compromise his beliefs. He will not forgive or forget anyone who has wronged him.

Stellium in Scorpio (Sun, Mercury, Venus, Jupiter)- He is emotionally intense and obsessed with matters related to death, sex, and psycho-spirituality. He has abandonment issues, which is why he is obsessive and controlling in relationships. He can be vengeful and unforgiving.

Planets and points in the houses

Stellium in the 8th house- He is innately drawn to the darker, taboo aspects of life, including sex, death, and psychoanalysis. People are inexplicable attracted to him. He tends to be private and secretive, so no one ever knows the real him.

Aquarius in the 11th house- He finds emotional security through groups of friends. He feels the need to belong to a community of like-minded people with radical, different ideas.

Discussion:

Charles Manson is clearly defined by his Scorpio stellium in the 8th house of sex and death. He used his magnetic personality to lure in followers, then manipulated them to exert his need for total dominance and control. His overbearing Scorpio nature, combined with the grandiose plans of his Moon in Aquarius, contributed to creating the monster that he became.

Scorpio Serial Killer 2: Derrick Todd Lee

Nickname: *The Baton Rouge Serial Killer*

He was named after the area in which he committed his crimes.

Biography:

Derrick Todd Lee was born on November 5, 1968, in St. Francisville, Louisiana, in the United States. His parents were Samuel Ruth and Florence Lee. He had three siblings (Montaldo, 2019).

His father left the family when Derrick was still young. This turned out to be a blessing in disguise, as Samuel had a history of mental illness, and was later institutionalized for the attempted murder of his ex-wife.

Florence Lee eventually married Coleman Barrow. They insisted their children get a good education and strictly adhere to the Bible. Coleman physically abused Derrick, and he was bossed by his domineering mother.

Derrick Lee's IQ was calculated to be below 75, which made it difficult for him to keep up with normal academic requirements. At school, he was bullied and abused by both schoolmates and adults who referred to him as dim-witted or retarded. His only interest was playing in the school band.

To compensate for the abuse that he received, Derrick would routinely torture small animals. Even though he was put in remedial education classes, Derrick only completed ten years of schooling. He was awarded a General Education Diploma (GED).

In 1988, he met and married Jacqueline Simms. They had two children. The marriage was not a happy one, as Lee abused Simms, and had numerous extramarital affairs. He frequented local bars to drink and pick up women.

According to family members, Simms lived in fear of Lee, and against her wishes, he had his mistress move into their home.

Crime Review:

Derrick Todd Lee's criminal behavior started when he was only 11 years old. He was caught peeping into a St. Francisville woman's home. This would be the first of many such offenses, a fetish he never outgrew.

By the time he was 18, Lee's criminal record included arrests for stalking, peeping into homes, break-in, and burglary, among other crimes. In 1983, he was arrested on a murder charge, but released due to lack of evidence.

It is unclear what drove Derrick Todd Lee over the edge to start his killing spree. His first known victim was Randi Mebruer, who disappeared in April 1998. Later, the death of Eugene Boisfontaine, who was beaten to death on June 1, 1997, was also linked to Lee.

Here is a tentative timeline of Derrick Todd Lee's known and possible crimes:

- *November 8, 1981-* Burglary of a shop and assault on an unknown victim.

- *Sometime in 1985-* Suspected of killing an unknown person.

- *August 8, 1985-* Set a car on fire.

- *August 1985-* Threatened to kill his father-in-law with a gun.

- *August 23, 1992-* Suspected of killing Connie Warner with a hammer.

- *January 1, 1993-* Robbed and assault Melvin Foster.

- *April 4, 1993-* Battered a teenage couple.

- *September 24, 1993-* Burgled a receiving depot of a charity.

- *June 1, 1997-* Assaulted and killed Eugenie Boisfontaine.

- *April 18, 1998-* Raped, stabbed, and beat Randi Mebruer to death. Her body has not been found.

- *June 1, 1999-* Colette Walker charged Lee with stalking.

- *January 22, 2000-* Assaulted his girlfriend and tried to kill a police deputy.

- *September 24, 2001-* Raped and strangled Gina Wilson Green.

- *September 26, 2002-* Suspected of beating up his wife.

- *January 24, 2002-* Killed Geralyn DeSoto after assaulting, raping, and knifing her.

- *May 23, 2002-* Suspected of battering Christine Moore to death.

- *July 9, 2002-* Attempted to rape and kill Diane Alexander.

- *July 12, 2002-* Cut the throat of Pamela Kilmore after raping her.

- *November 21, 2002-* Raped and beat Dene Colomb to death.

- *December 25, 2002-* Suspected of killing Mary Ann Fowler, who disappeared.

- *March 3, 2003-* Assaulted, raped, and smothered Carrie Lynn Yoder.

The murder method varied with each case. The only similarity between the crimes was the removal of phones from the victim's belongings and the lack of forced entry. Most of the murders were committed near Louisiana State University (LSU). Two bodies were found in Whiskey Bay.

Public hysteria created rumors which hindered the case. In early 2003, an urban legend began to circulate that Lee was using the taped sounds of a crying baby to lure victims to the door. This was proven to be untrue.

Because of an erroneous FBI suspect profile and unreliable eyewitness accounts, initially the police were looking for a white perpetrator. Police administered thousands of DNA tests to Caucasian men in and around the general area of the murders.

When this approach generated no leads, police allowed a company called DNAPrint Genomics to access DNA left at the crime scenes. They generated a profile indicating the suspect was 85% African, which changed the course of the investigation.

Armed with this new DNA evidence and a description provided by a survivor, Lee was positively identified. Police issued an arrest warrant for Lee, who fled to Chicago and then Atlanta in an effort to escape murder charges. He was finally captured in Atlanta, Georgia, in May 2003.

The Baton Rouge police came under heavy criticism for their handling of the case. Lee had been arrested numerous times during his killing spree for unrelated offenses. Considering Lee's extensive criminal history, residents were shocked he was never a suspect.

There was some argument that because of his low IQ, Lee was incompetent to stand trial. Despite these objections, the trials against him moved forward. In 2004, Lee was convicted of the murders of Geralyn DeSoto and Charlotte Murray Pace. For the first murder, he was sentenced to life imprisonment; for the second, to be executed.

Derrick Todd Lee died from unspecified heart disease on January 21, 2016.

Overview of Birth Chart

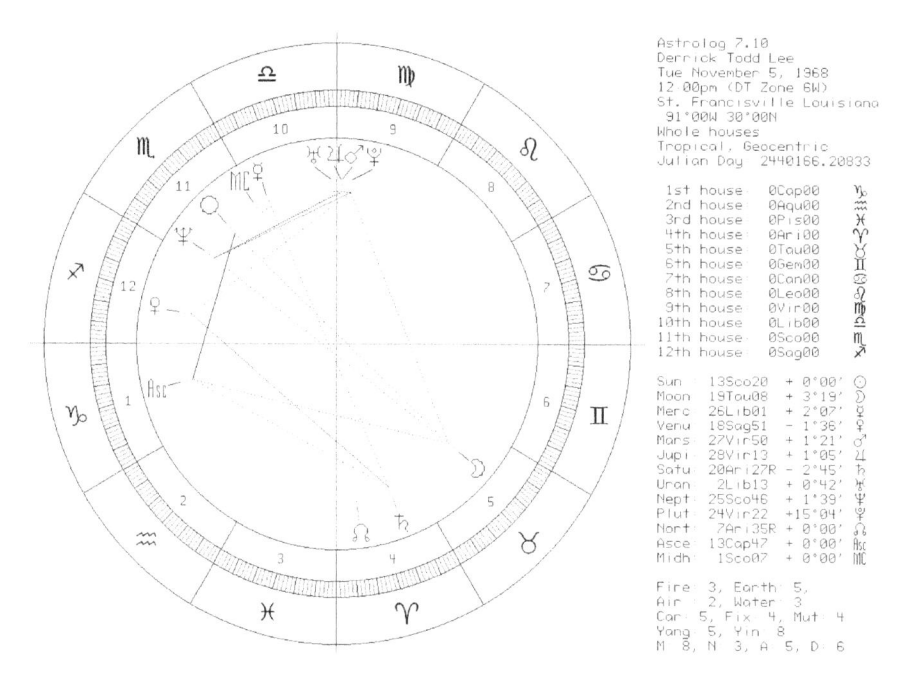

```
Astrolog 7.10
Derrick Todd Lee
Tue November 5, 1968
12:00pm (DT Zone 6W)
St. Francisville Louisiana
91°00W 30°00N
Whole houses
Tropical, Geocentric
Julian Day  2440166.20833

1st house    0Cap00
2nd house    0Aqu00
3rd house    0Pis00
4th house    0Ari00
5th house    0Tau00
6th house    0Gem00
7th house    0Can00
8th house    0Leo00
9th house    0Vir00
10th house   0Lib00
11th house   0Sco00
12th house   0Sag00

Sun   13Sco20  + 0°00'
Moon  19Tau08  + 3°19'
Merc  26Lib01  + 2°07'
Venu  18Sag51  - 1°36'
Mars  27Vir50  + 1°21'
Jupi  29Vir13  + 1°05'
Satu  20Ari27R - 2°45'
Uran   2Lib13  + 0°42'
Nept  25Sco46  + 1°39'
Plut  24Vir22  +15°04'
Nort   7Ari35R + 0°00'
Asce  13Cap47  + 0°00'
Midh   1Sco07  + 0°00'

Fire  3, Earth  5,
Air   2, Water  3
Car   5, Fix    4, Mut  4
Yang  5, Yin    8
M  8, N  3, A  5, D  6
```

<u>Derrick Todd Lee - November 5, 1968</u>

Planets and points in the signs

Sun in Scorpio- Intense and complex by nature, he has extremely strong emotional reactions to most situations. Feelings are often very difficult for him to verbalize.

Mars in Virgo- He is insecure and self-critical. He becomes frustrated when things are out of his control.

Stellium in Virgo (Mars, Jupiter, Pluto)- He is highly stubborn and critical of himself as well as others. He does not handle change well and thrives on routine and stability.

133

Discussion:

The intense, dark emotions from his Sun in Scorpio and the painful self-loathing from his Virgo stellium were not a good mix for Derrick Todd Lee. When combined with a family history of mental illness, he didn't stand a chance.

Shared Pointers From the Natal Chart Reports

Both killers share the Sun in Scorpio and Mars in Virgo. Their emotional reactions are very intense, subjected to their unconscious mind which is in turn dictated by childhood experiences. They are inclined to take things to the extreme. When this includes a desperate need to be in control, the end results can be disastrous.

Chapter 9: Sagittarius

(November 22 - December 21)
Modality - Mutable
Element - Fire

Sagittarius Personality Traits

Half-man, half-horse, Sagittarius has a dual nature. As the archer, their feet are planted on the ground while they shoot for the stars. They have the following positive attributes:

- They are good-humored, cheerful, and live life to the fullest.

- They are outspoken and will tell you the truth, even if you are not prepared to receive it.

- They are independent with an affinity for the outdoors.

- Sagittarians stay detached and thoughtful, away from life's realities.

- They are confident in their abilities.

- They are matter-of-fact and will not mislead or flatter other people just to shield them from unpleasant happenings and facts.

- Sagittarians are easy-going and friendly.

- They are intelligent, philosophical, idealistic, and need to be careful to avoid being lured into narrow viewpoints.

Sagittarians also share the following negative characteristics:

- They can be insensitive and inconsiderate in their handling of honest communication.

- Sagittarians can be reckless and heedless of the consequences of their actions.

- With a tendency to exaggerate and glorify certain aspects, they are prone to falling victim to dogmas and creeds with a narrow vision.

- Being indiscreet and incautious without learning balance and wisdom can reinforce the vulnerability of becoming fanatics.

- They are restive, fidgety, and interested in new and idealistic philosophies and approaches.

Sagittarius is the sign of <u>mutable</u> <u>fire</u>. This combination leads to their general restlessness and idealistic behavior. The fire of Sagittarius burns like a wildfire, unpredictable and spreading out in all directions.

Fire gives Sagittarians infinite energy, while their mutable modality propels them to wander and wonder restlessly, gathering and sharing knowledge and wisdom. They are charismatic and thrive on adventure, always on the lookout for their next thrill.

Sagittarius Serial Killer 1: Ted Bundy

Nickname: The Lady Killer

The nickname refers to the fact that Ted Bundy regarded himself as irresistible to women.

Biography:

Ted Bundy was born on November 24, 1946, to Eleanor Louise Cowell at a home for unwed mothers in Burlington, Vermont, in the United States. The identity of his biological father remains unknown.

As a toddler, Ted was raised by his deeply religious grandparents in order to neutralize the shame and social stigma that would be attached to his mother as a single parent. He grew up believing his grandparents were his parents and his mother was his older sister. This led to a lifelong resentment and bitterness toward his mother for never telling him the truth about his parentage.

Ted's grandfather was a tyrant and a bigot who hated blacks, Italians, Catholics, and Jews. Prone to violent rages, he would beat his wife and the family dog, and once threw his daughter down the stairs for oversleeping. Ted's grandmother was a timid woman who underwent electroshock therapy for depression. Bundy started showing strange behaviors quite early in life, including a fascination with knives.

In 1950, Ted and his mother moved to Tacoma, Washington, where she married Johnny Bundy a year later. They had four children together. Bundy adopted Ted as his own and tried to include him in family activities, but Ted never showed much respect for his step-father. He looked down on him for being uneducated and working class *(Sullivan, 2020)*.

There are different accounts of Ted Bundy's adolescent years. In various interviews, he claimed he remained alone and did not understand how to enter into friendship and romantic relations. However, classmates recalled him as a sociable and well-liked person who was moderately successful in romantic encounters.

As a teenager, Ted started abusing alcohol and peeping through women's windows to watch them undress. He enjoyed skiing and would steal ski equipment and forge lift tickets.

In 1965, Ted graduated from high school and attended various universities until he finally received a degree in psychology from the University of Washington in 1972. While an undergraduate, he worked on a number of political campaigns in different capacities. His co-workers described him as "smart, aggressive, and a believer in the system."

As a student at the University of Washington in 1967, Bundy fell in love with a fellow student from California. He identified her by the pseudonym Stephanie Brooks. In 1968, Brooks broke off their relationship because of Ted's lack of ambition. It devastated him. A psychiatrist later pinpointed this rejection as a pivotal point that led towards his subsequent killing spree. Many of Bundy's victims resembled his college girlfriend— attractive students with long, dark hair.

Ted Bundy met Elizabeth Kloepfer in 1969, and they began a stormy off-and-on-again relationship that extended well past his first arrests and imprisonment.

By the mid-1970s, Bundy appeared to have turned his life around. In 1973, he was accepted into the law schools of the Universities of Puget Sound and Utah based on recommendations from his political connections. He contacted Brooks again, and she was amazed at his change to a serious professional. They resumed dating; he even introduced Brooks to colleagues as his fiancé.

Then, in January 1974, Bundy abruptly cut off all ties, refusing to return Brooks' phone calls or letters. He never provided a reason. Brooks later concluded Bundy deliberately planned the entire engagement and rejection as retribution for the breakup she initiated in 1968.

The entire time Bundy was engaged to Brooks, he was also secretly dating Kloepfer. Unbeknownst to either of the two women, Bundy had started skipping classes at law school. By April 1974, he stopped attending entirely. It was around this time young women began to disappear in the Pacific Northwest.

Crime Review:

During high school, Bundy was arrested at least twice on suspicion of burglary and auto theft, but his juvenile records were expunged when he turned 18. There is indirect evidence he may have abducted and killed an eight-year-old girl when he was 14.

It is not known when Ted began his murdering career. Over the years, he confessed and retracted different crimes to various people. He alleged that he kidnapped and killed two women in Atlantic City in 1969, and another in 1971 in Seattle.

Bundy's first confirmed crime occurred shortly after midnight on January 4, 1974, around the same time he ended his relationship with Brooks. He assaulted a young female student and dancer, beating her senseless with a metal rod. She survived, but with permanent mental and physical disabilities.

In the first six months of 1974, female college students in the Pacific Northwest started disappearing at a rate of about one per month. Witnesses described a man with his arm in a sling or a leg cast requesting help to carry a case to his car.

The victims were all young female students wearing jeans or slacks, with long hair parted in the middle. The attacks were at night, near construction sites, and witnesses described a man with a cast or sling and driving a tan or beige Volkswagen Beetle.

His last two Washington abductions took place in broad daylight at a crowded beach at Lake Sammamish State Park in Issaquah, about a 20-minute drive east of Seattle. Witnesses provided the same description as the night killings.

Armed with a detailed description of the suspect and his car, King County police released a composite sketch to Seattle-area newspapers and media outlets. Several people - including Bundy's girlfriend, Elizabeth Kloepfer - recognized and identified Ted as the killer. However, detectives dismissed these tips, thinking a law student with no previous criminal record was an unlikely suspect.

The victims officially attributed to Bundy in Washington/Oregon are:

- *January 1974*- Karen Sparks, 18. She was beaten with a metal rod but survived.

- *February 1974*- Lynda Ann Healey, 21. Her skull was found on Taylor Mountain 14 months after her disappearance.

- *March 1974*- Donna Gail Manson, 19. Her body was never found, but Bundy claimed to have burned her skull in Kloepfer's fireplace.

- *April 1974*- Susan Elaine Rancourt, 18. Disappeared from the campus of Central Washington State College, east of Seattle. One of Bundy's few blonde victims.

- *May 1974*- Roberta Kathleen Parks, 20. The first known victim in Oregon, her skull was also found on Taylor Mountain.

- *June 1974*- Brenda Carol Ball, 22. Her skull was found on Taylor Mountain.

- *June 1974*- Georgann Hawkins, 18. Her body has never been recovered.

- *July 1974*- Janice Ann Ott, 23, and Denise Marie Naslund, 19. Both kidnapped in on the same day from the state park beach in Issaquah.

In August 1974, Ted Bundy was accepted into the University of Utah Law School and moved to Salt Lake City, where he started his new killing spree. At his trial, Bundy described in detail the macabre rituals he performed with each corpse, including shampooing their hair and applying makeup.

His victims in Utah/Colorado/Idaho were:

- *October 1974-* Nancy Wilcox, 16. She went out to buy a pack of gum and was never seen again.

- *October 1974-* Rhonda Stapley. She managed to escape by jumping into a nearby river. Fearing public ridicule, she didn't come forward with her story until 2011, nearly forty years later.

- *October 1974-* Melissa Ann Smith, 17. The daughter of a local police chief, her body was found in Summit Park, in the mountains east of Salt Lake City.

- *October 1974-* Laura Ann Aime, 17. Hikers found her frozen body in the mountains about a month later.

- *November 1974-* Carol DaRonch, 18. Bundy lured her into his car by posing as a police officer. She escaped when he failed to properly secure her handcuffs.

- *November 1974-* Debi Kent, 17. Only hours after DaRonch's escape, Bundy succeeded in abducting Debi Kent after a high school play in Bountiful, Utah.

After reading about the disappearances in the Salt Lake City area, Kloepfer contacted King County police a second time. In December, she also called the Salt Lake County Sheriff's Office. They added Bundy to their list of suspects, but without concrete forensic evidence, they had nothing to link him to the crimes.

In January 1975, Bundy briefly returned to Washington and spent a week with Kloepfer. She did not tell him she had reported him to the police three times.

In 1975, Bundy shifted his operations to Colorado. His victims there were:

- *January 1975-* Caryn Eileen Campbell, 23. She disappeared from the hotel lobby while vacationing with her fiancé in Aspen.

- *March 1975-* Julie Cunningham, 26. A local ski instructor, Bundy approached her on crutches, pretending to need help.

- *April 1975-* Denise Lynn Oliverson, 24. She was riding her bicycle to her parents' house and never arrived. Her bike was found under a viaduct.

- *May 1975-* Lynette Culver, 12. One of Bundy's youngest victims. He threw her body into a river. It was never recovered.

- *June 1975-* Susan Curtis, 15. Disappeared while attending a Mormon youth conference. Her body was never found.

On August 16, 1975, Bundy was arrested by Utah Highway Patrol for cruising a residential neighborhood in pre-dawn hours. They searched his car and found a ski mask, another mask fashioned from pantyhose, a crowbar, handcuffs, trash bags, a coil of rope, an ice pick, and various burglary tools.

Police questioned Bundy and searched his apartment, but failed to find the collection of Polaroids he had taken of his victims. Without sufficient evidence to keep Bundy in custody, he was released on his own recognizance.

In September, Bundy sold his Volkswagen Beetle and police impounded it. They found hairs inside the car belonging to three of the missing women. Carol DaRonch, the girl who had escaped from his bungled abduction attempt, positively identified him, as did witnesses from the school in Bountiful.

Thirty police detectives from five different states pooled their investigations, but determined they still didn't have enough evidence to charge Bundy with the murders.

In February 1976, Ted Bundy was sentenced to 1-to-15 years in Utah prison for kidnapping Carol DaRonch. He escaped in June 1977, but was apprehended within a few days. Back in prison, Bundy sawed a hole in the reinforced ceiling of his cell and escaped a second time. This time he managed to flee to Florida.

In January 1978, having been in Florida for less than a week. Ted Bundy broke into a Florida State University sorority house. He severely assaulted four young women, killing two of them.

His victims in Florida were:

- *January 1978-* Margaret Elizabeth Bowman, 21, and Lisa Levy, 20, were asleep in their beds when Bundy broke into their sorority house and attacked them. Two other girls in the sorority, Karen Chandler and Kathy Kleiner, survived.

- *January 1978-* Cheryl Thomas, another FSU student who lived at an apartment nearby, also survived but was suffered permanent deafness.

- *February 1978-* Kimberly Leach, 12. Bundy's final victim. She was kidnapped from around her school in Lake City, Florida. Her body was found two months later, 35 miles away in Suwannee River State Park.

Bundy was arrested by a Pensacola police officer on February 12, 1978, when he recognized the car Bundy was driving was stolen. In separate trials, Ted Bundy was sentenced to death three times for the severity of his crimes. He confessed to 30 murders, but his true body count is thought to be much higher — possibly 100 or more.

After his conviction, Ted Bundy was interviewed extensively and made many conflicting confessions. He married a former co-worker, Elizabeth Boone, while in jail. They had a child together.

Ted Bundy was executed in Florida on January 24, 1989.

Overview of Birth Chart

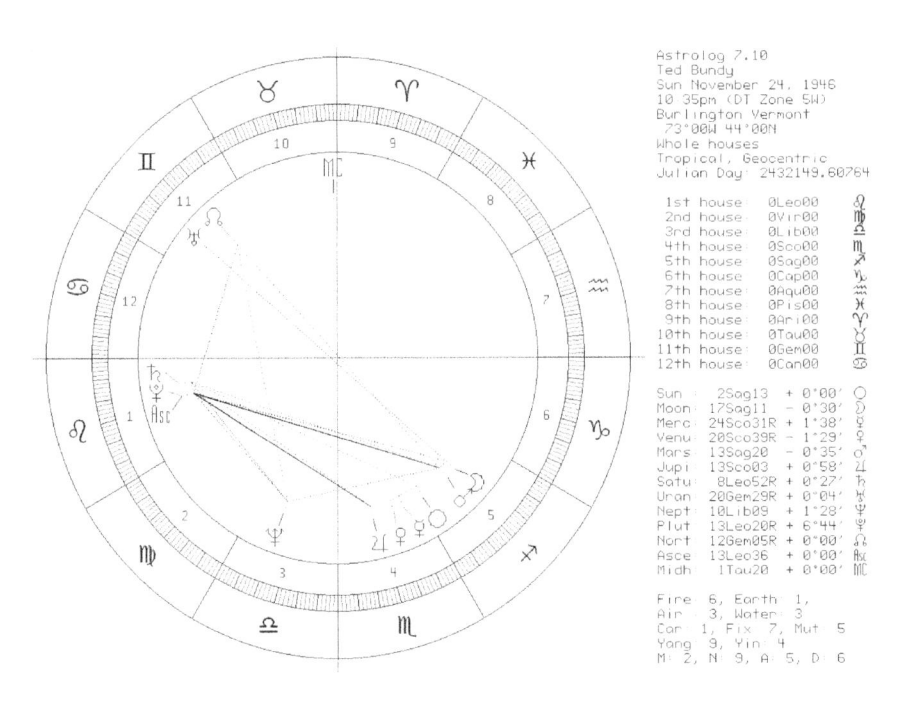

Ted Bundy - November 24, 1946

Planets and points in the signs

Moon in Sagittarius- He can be intolerant, closed-minded, dogmatic, arrogant, non-objective, risk-taking, and possess a holier-than-thou attitude.

Mercury in Scorpio- He is secretive and introverted, and finds it difficult to open up. He has a hard time dealing with people. He has no qualms with contradicting himself and may come across as dishonest.

Venus in Scorpio- When he loves, it may lead to jealousy and absolute exclusivity, bordering on the will to control his partner. He has abandonment issues, which is why he is obsessive and controlling in relationships.

Jupiter in Scorpio - He is secretive, detached, unforgiving, stubborn, sneaky. He does not forgive or forget.

Stellium in Sagittarius (Sun, Moon, Mars)- He is over-confident to the point of recklessness. He is easily bored and requires constant stimulation. He has a fiery temper and is quick to anger.

Stellium in Scorpio (Mercury, Venus, Jupiter)- He is clandestine and secretive. He has a magnetic personality and may use it to manipulate others. He is emotionally intense and obsessed with matters related to death and sex. He is possessive and controlling, and can be vengeful and unforgiving.

Planets and points in the houses

Leo in the 1st house- He can be arrogant, quick-tempered, and prone to drama. If someone attacks his pride, he feels so hurt and humiliated that he seldom forgives them. He'll do anything to attract attention.

Stellium in 4th house- He is heavily influenced by his childhood and has a strong connection to his family, roots, and heritage.

Stellium in 5th house- He has a flair for the theatrical and is prone to drama. He craves being around important people.

Discussion:

With a Scorpio stellium in his 4th house of home and family, it's no wonder that Ted Bundy never forgave his mother for deceiving him about his true parentage. This would have been the first major betrayal in his life; the second was his college girlfriend's rejection. In true Scorpio fashion, he carefully plotted out his revenge. When a stellium is over-energized, it can active the opposite house. It's no wonder Bundy leveraged his law career in order to manipulate people - the 4th house of home is polar opposites to the 10th house of work.

Sagittarius is one of the most emotionally cold signs of the Zodiac, and this stellium in the 5th house of creativity can lead to Machiavellian tendencies.

In Bundy, these two extreme stelliums manifested as intense desires, obsession, and destructiveness. He took out his revenge upon all females by killing them.

> *"When you feel the last bit of breath leaving their body, you're looking into their eyes. A person in that situation is God!"*
>
> *- Ted Bundy*

Sagittarius Serial Killer 2: Edmund Kemper

Nickname: The Co-Ed Killer

His nickname stems from the fact that he mostly killed young female students.

Biography:

Edmund Emil Kemper III was born on December 18, 1948, in Burbank, California, in the United States. His parents were Edmund Emil Kemper II and Clarnell Elizabeth Kemper. He was a middle child with two sisters, the elder of which was particularly abusive to him.

Edmund II was a veteran of the Second World War and participated in the first nuclear tests. After his return, he worked as an electrician. His wife was critical of him and his work and often complained about his small earnings and the low social status (in her eyes) of his job.

Following a turbulent marriage, the Kempers divorced in 1957. Clarnell moved to Montana with the children. Edmund was very close to his father, so the separation devastated him (Frasier & Newton, 2007).

Edmund's mother was an unbalanced alcoholic who abused and humiliated him. She locked him in the basement of the home at night because she was afraid he might try to rape his sisters. His elder sister nearly killed him twice: once when she pushed him in front of a train, and again when she tried to drown him.

Edmund was of above-average intelligence but started showing signs of excessive cruelty at an early age. At 10, he killed the family cat by first burying it alive, then decapitating it, and displaying the head on a spike. He stabbed a second cat to death, his younger sister's favorite, and cut it into pieces, which he kept in his closet.

He would act out dark fantasies involving ritualistic games in which he would decapitate his sisters' dolls, or role-play about being executed in the electric chair or gas chamber.

Edmund was always big for his age; at 15, he was already 6 foot 4 inches tall. His mother would mock and deride him because of his height, calling him "a real weirdo."

When he was 14 years old, he ran away from home to find his father in California. There he discovered that his father had remarried and replaced Edmund with a stepson. Edmund was heartbroken.

Edmund's father sent him to live with his paternal grandparents on their ranch in North Fork, California. He came to hate his grandparents and described them as senile. Edmund especially despised his grandmother, who he felt was constantly emasculating him and his grandfather.

Crime Review:

In August 1964, at the age of 15, Edmund Kemper had a nasty quarrel with his grandmother and shot her with a hunting rifle. When his grandfather returned from shopping,

Edmund also shot and killed him. After calling his mother, he turned himself in.

During psychiatric tests, he was identified as a paranoid schizophrenic and was sent to Atascadero State Hospital for the Criminally Insane. A psychiatrist theorized he was avenging the rejection of both his father and mother.

At the hospital, Edmund gained the trust of the hospital staff and was even allowed to administer tests to other patients, including sex offenders. He was paroled on his 21st birthday, in December 1969. Although hospital personnel advised against it, Edmund was released into the custody of his mother. It was a toxic and hostile environment, and they frequently had vicious, heated arguments.

Edmund began attending community college as part of his parole requirements and hoped to become a police officer. But at 6 foot 9 inches, he was disqualified from joining the force because he was too tall. He started working for the California Division of Highways and was finally able to buy a car and move out of his mother's apartment.

During this time, he noticed many female students were hitchhiking in the area. He equipped his car with plastic bags, knives, handcuffs, blankets, and other equipment. It is estimated he picked up over 150 young female hitchhikers, but he let them all go without injury. That all changed in May 1972, when he began acting on his homicidal sexual urges.

Between May 1972 and April 1973, Edmund is known to have murdered at least eight people in Northern California. His method involved picking up young women, who he took to remote areas and shot, stabbed, strangled, or smothered. After the killing, he would bring their bodies home, cut off their heads, commit necrophilia, and dismember the body.

His six young female victims were:

- *May 7, 1972-* Mary Ann Pesce, 18, and Anita Mary Luchessa, 18, students from Fresno State University. Both were strangled and fatally stabbed, then dismembered and decapitated. Pesce's head was discovered in the woods near Santa Cruz. Luchessa's remains have never been found.

- *September 14, 1972-* Aiko Koo, 15, a dance student who decided to hitchhike after she missed her bus. He fatally strangled her with her scarf; engaged in necrophilia, then dissected her body, removing her head and hands.

- *January 7, 1973-* Cindy Schall, 18, from Cabrillo College. He shot her in the head with a .22 pistol; engaged in necrophilia with her corpse, then dissected and dismembered her. He buried her skull in his mother's garden and tossed the rest of her remains off a cliff into the ocean. Over the following weeks, most of the pieces were retrieved when they washed back to shore.

- *February 5, 1973-* Rosalind Heather Thorpe, 23, and Alice Helen Liu, 20, from the University of California, Santa Cruz, where Edmund's mother worked. They trusted him because he has a UCSC sticker on his car. He shot them both with a .22 pistol; engaged in necrophilia with their bodies, then dismembered them at his mother's house. Their remains were discovered by hikers near Highway 1 in San Mateo County.

Finally, on April 20, 1973, Edmund waited until his mother fell asleep; he proceeded to kill her with a hammer and slit her throat. He cut out her tongue and vocal cords as a final act of revenge for years of verbal abuse. He performed necrophilia on her corpse, then went to a nearby bar.

Upon returning home, he invited Sally Hallett, his mother's best friend, over for dinner and a movie. When she arrived, he strangled her and stashed her body in a closet. Edmund drove to Pueblo, Colorado, where he turned himself over to the police.

Edmund Kemper was indicted on eight counts of first-degree murder on May 7, 1973. During his trial, he was assessed as legally sane. He requested to be sentenced to death and executed by electrical chair, like he used to play-act as a child. But the state of California had temporarily suspended capital punishment, denying him his childhood fantasy.

Edmund Kemper is currently serving eight concurrent life sentences at the California Medical Facility in Vacaville. He is next eligible for parole in 2024.

"If I killed them, you know, they couldn't reject me as a man. It was more or less making a doll out of a human being . . . and carrying out my fantasies with a doll, a living human doll."

–Edmund Kemper

Overview of Birth Chart

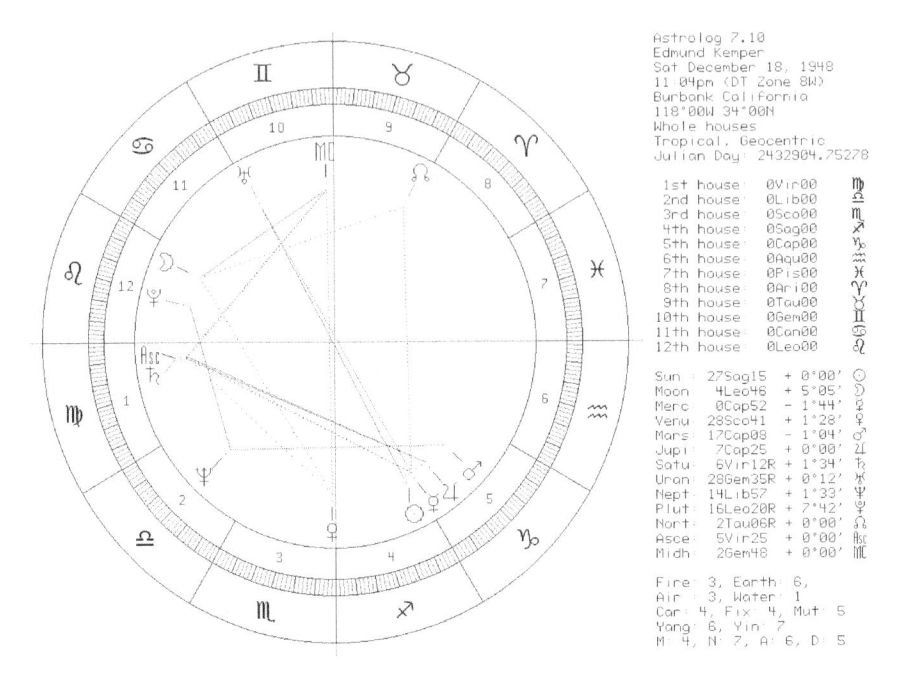

```
Astrolog 7.10
Edmund Kemper
Sat December 18, 1948
11:04pm (DT Zone 8W)
Burbank California
118°00W 34°00N
Whole houses
Tropical, Geocentric
Julian Day: 2432904.75278

1st house:   0Vir00   ♍
2nd house:   0Lib00   ♎
3rd house:   0Sco00   ♏
4th house:   0Sag00   ♐
5th house:   0Cap00   ♑
6th house:   0Aqu00   ♒
7th house:   0Pis00   ♓
8th house:   0Ari00   ♈
9th house:   0Tau00   ♉
10th house:  0Gem00   ♊
11th house:  0Can00   ♋
12th house:  0Leo00   ♌

Sun : 27Sag15  + 0°00'  ☉
Moon:  4Leo46  + 5°05'  ☽
Merc:  0Cap52  - 1°44'  ☿
Venu: 28Sco41  + 1°28'  ♀
Mars: 17Cap08  - 1°04'  ♂
Jupi:  7Cap25  + 0°00'  ♃
Satu:  6Vir12R + 1°34'  ♄
Uran: 28Gem35R + 0°12'  ♅
Nept: 14Lib57  + 1°33'  ♆
Plut: 16Leo20R + 7°42'  ♇
Nort:  2Tau06R + 0°00'  ☊
Asce:  5Vir25  + 0°00'  Asc
Midh:  2Gem48  + 0°00'  MC

Fire: 3, Earth: 6,
Air : 3, Water: 1
Car: 4, Fix: 4, Mut: 5
Yang: 6, Yin: 7
M: 4, N: 7, A: 6, D: 5
```

<u>Edmund Kemper - December 18, 1948</u>

Planets and points in the signs

Sun in Sagittarius- He has a quick temper. He can be blunt and hurtful.

Moon in Leo- He can be bossy and overbearing, with a need to control people and things around him. He is prone to melodrama if he doesn't get his way.

Venus in Scorpio- His feelings about others are deep and powerful. Because his feelings are so complex and intense, they may frighten him—so he often tries to ignore them. But the more he does, the more explosive things get when he eventually does express them.

Jupiter in Capricorn- He is very systematic. He has a thirst for power and a selfish nature.

Stellium in Capricorn (Mercury, Mars, Jupiter)- He can be pessimistic and overly critical of himself and the world around him. He is stubborn and controlling. It's easy for him to get caught up in a cycle of negativity and mood swings. He has strong family ties.

Pluto in Leo- He needs power and control. He has quite a temper and can throw a nasty tantrum if he doesn't get what he wants.

Planets and points in the houses

Sun in 4th house- He is motivated by domestic and family concerns. A peaceful home life is very important to him. He is obsessed with family and has a strong need to be loved by those closest to him.

Stellium in 5th house- He has a strong inner child and a need to play. He is creative and theatrical. He may be prone to gambling or other risk-taking ventures.

Discussion:

Edmund Kemper's natal chart indicates a strong attachment to family and a desperate need to be loved. The double betrayal by his parents, as well as his sister's attempts to kill him, would have left a lasting negative impact on him.

The Capricorn stellium in his 5th house of play and self-expression is especially chilling. He never outgrew his dark childhood game of dismembering dolls. Instead, he turned his unfortunate victims into playthings for his own twisted amusement. It seems only fitting that the court denied him his final childhood fantasy - to be executed.

Shared Pointers From the Natal Chart Reports

Ted Bundy and Edmund Kemper share many pointers on their natal charts - Sun in Sagittarius, Venus in Scorpio, Uranus in Gemini, Neptune in Libra, and Pluto in Leo. The slower-moving outer planets (Uranus, Neptune, and Pluto) appear in the charts of everyone born in the mid-to-late 1940s, the so-called "Baby Boomer" generation.

Their shared Venus in Scorpio indicates powerful and intense feelings; while the shared stelliums in the 5th house give a flair for the dramatic. Both had resentments and problems stemming from maternal problems, which manifested in their killing of females as a surrogate for killing their mothers.

Chapter 10: Capricorn

(December 22 - January 19)
Modality - Cardinal
Element - Earth

Capricorn Personality Traits

Capricorn is considered by some astrologers to be the strongest sign of the Zodiac. The outstanding traits of Capricorns are:

- The masters of discipline, they show endurance and restraint.

- They are sensible and careful in any endeavor that they undertake.

- Ambition leads them to aspire to be leaders; they do not function well in lesser positions.

- The hallmark of Capricorns is pragmatism and hands-on leadership.

- They set clear goals and the rules for achieving them.

- Capricorns believe that rewards and punishments should be associated with success or failure.

- A good sense of humor tempers some of the harsher aspects of the Capricorn's makeup.

- They are normally restrained and self-contained in their interactions with other people.

- They are diligent and methodical, leading to the successful completion of any pursuit.

- Capricorns are hard-working people.

The characteristics of Capricorns can also lead to less desirable attributes:

- They can become cynical and depressed if activities do not work out as planned.

- Due to their restrained nature, they can be reluctant and hesitant in interactions with other people.

- Capricorns can become fatalistic and believe that nothing can change the outcome of situations.

- In their pursuit to complete endeavors, they can become relentless task-masters.

- They are frugal and may withhold resources to others in need.

- They want to be completely self-sufficient and may feel lonely and isolated as a result.

As the sign of <u>cardinal</u> <u>earth</u>, Capricorns are the initiators and planners. Firmly grounded in reality, they set definite goals which they pursue with discipline and patience. They have a formidable presence and are natural authority figures.

Capricorn Serial Killer 1: Harold Shipman

Nickname: Doctor Death

He was named by the media after it came to light he killed hundreds of his patients.

Biography:

Harold Frederick "Fred" Shipman was born on January 14, 1946, in Nottingham, England. His father was a truck driver, also named Harold Frederick Shipman. His mother, Vera Brittan Shipman, was a housewife. His parents were devout Methodists *(Kaplan, 2010)*.

The second of four children, Fred was his mother's clear favorite. Her favoritism gave him a sense of superiority, which left him isolated as a child, with few friends. He was a good student and sportsman. He excelled at rugby and long-distance running, and served as vice-captain of the athletics team.

When his mother was diagnosed with lung cancer, Fred helped care for her during her lengthy illness. He grew especially fascinated by the morphine the physician administered at home, and how it relieved her pain. He was 17 when she finally died in 1963. Devastated by her death, he resolved to become a doctor.

In 1966, at the age of 19, Fred married 17-year-old Primrose Mary Oxtoby who was five-months pregnant. They would go on to have four children.

He attended medical school at Leeds University and graduated in 1970. After graduation, he was employed at the Pontefract General Infirmary in Yorkshire. He then transferred to Abraham Ormerod Medical Centre in Todmorden as a general practitioner (GP).

While at the clinic in Todmorden, Shipman became addicted to the painkiller, Pethidine. In 1975, he was caught forging prescriptions for his own personal use. He was fined and sent to a drug rehabilitation clinic in York.

In 1977, he moved to the Donneybrook Medical Centre in Hyde, near Manchester. For almost two decades, Shipmen worked in Hyde, earning a reputation as a hardworking doctor. While the junior staff found his behavior arrogant, he was widely trusted by patients and colleagues alike.

In 1983, he appeared in an interview on Granada Television about the treatment of people with mental health problems in the community.

Crime Review:

A local undertaker was the first to notice Dr. Shipman's patients seemed to be dying at an unusually high rate. He approached Shipman about it directly, but was assured there was nothing to be concerned about.

Then in 1998, Dr. Linda Reynolds of the Brooke Surgery in Hyde voiced similar concerns to John Pollard, the coroner of the South Manchester District. She was alarmed by the large number of cremation forms for elderly women.

Detectives opened an investigation but closed it on April 19, 1998 due to lack of evidence. Later, a more thorough analysis revealed Shipman had been altering his patients' medical records to corroborate their causes of death.

In August, taxi driver John Shaw independently told police he thought that Dr. Shipman was killing his patients. He was concerned by the number of otherwise healthy elderly ladies he transported to the hospital who suddenly died while in Dr. Shipman's care.

On June 24, 1998, Kathleen Grundy died at her home after Dr. Shipman visited her. Grundy's daughter, Angela Woodruff, was a lawyer who always handled her mother's affairs. She was surprised to learn a new will had been drawn up. It excluded Woodruff and her children and instead left the bulk of the estate to Dr. Shipman. Suspecting the new will was a forgery, Woodruff filed charges with the police.

Grundy's body was exhumed and found to contain traces of heroin. Dr. Shipman claimed Grundy was addicted to heroin and submitted entries into a computerized journal to support his claims. When the entries were scrutinized, they were shown to have been made after Grundy's death. Shipman's typewriter was identified as the machine used to draft the forged will.

On October 9th, Dr. Shipman charged with the murders of 15 women by lethal injections of diamorphine, all between 1995 and 1998. He was found guilty and sentenced to life imprisonment with a recommendation that he never should be considered for release.

After the trial, further investigations indicated Dr. Shipman may have killed up to 250 patients. His case led to a radical overview and change in medical procedures in order to prevent this from happening again.

On 13 January 2004, on the eve of his 58th birthday, Harold Shipman hanged himself in his jail cell.

Dr. Shipman's motives remain a matter of dispute. Some argue he was taking revenge for the death of his mother. Others believe he may have had a misguided sense to practice euthanasia.

Overview of Birth Chart

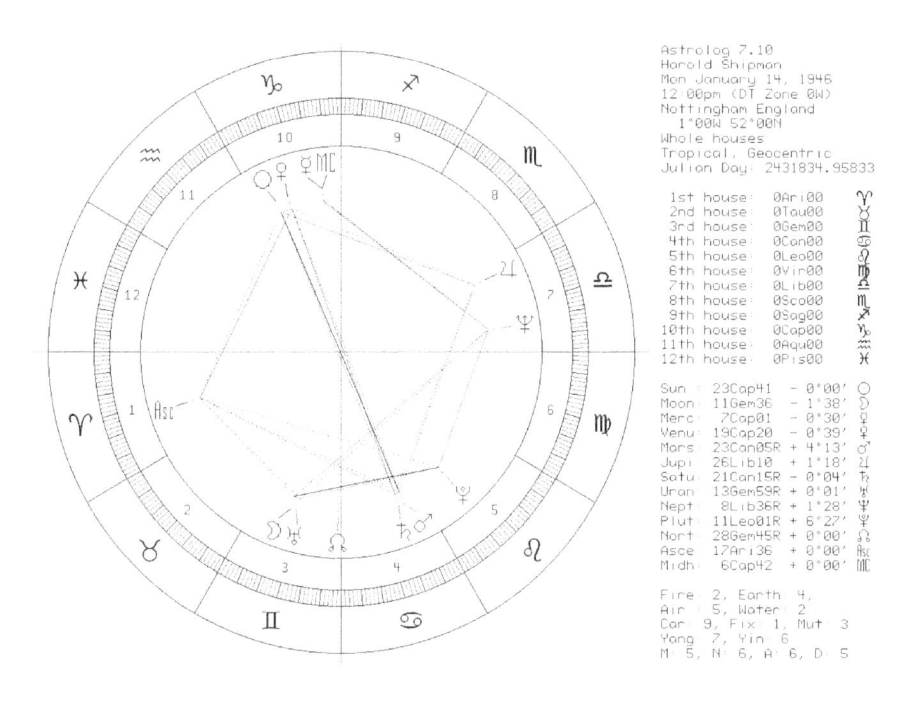

Harold Shipman - January 14, 1946

Planets and points in the signs

Sun in Capricorn- His quiet exterior makes him appear to be a loner. He builds a wall of reserve around him to protect himself from the ill winds of the world around him. Nothing gets in the way of his plans and ambitions.

Moon in Gemini- He tends to avoid deep emotional experiences, preferring a more logical, analytical approach.

Mercury in Capricorn- He comes across as cold and ambitious. People may find him arrogant and intolerant.

Mars in Cancer- He is highly protective of those he cares about. He uses emotional manipulation to get his way and can become passive-aggressive. He needs constant reassurance or he becomes depressed.

Saturn in Cancer- He is kind but may lack empathy. He can be so busy protecting himself from being hurt that he is unable to see the pain of others. He has a hard time letting go of the past.

Stellium in Capricorn (Sun, Mercury, Venus)- He is respected and admired by those he works with. He is ambitious and has a clear plan for his life. He can be stubborn and controlling. He may be overly critical of himself and the world around him. His nature is cold, calculating, and unemotional.

Discussion:

The prevalence of Cancer and the Capricorn stellium help explain the enigma that is Dr. Shipman. He was ambitious and rose to prominence in the medical field, only to be undone by his aloofness and lack of empathy. He did not understand why everybody was upset by the killings. He thought he was providing the world a service. The passing of his mother at such a young age had a life-altering impact on his personality.

Capricorn Serial Killer 2: Dean Corll

Nickname: The Candy Man

Corll was known as the Candy Man or the Pied Piper because his family owned a sweet factory. He was known to give free candy to local children.

Biography:

Dean Arnold Corll was born on December 24, 1939, in Fort Wayne, Indiana, in the United States. His father was Arnold Edwin Corll and his mother was Mary Emma Corll. He had one younger brother. Arnold was a strict disciplinarian, resorting to harsh punishment for even minor infractions. Mary was very protective towards her sons. The couple divorced in 1946 but remained on a friendly basis.

After Arnold was drafted into the United States Army, Mary relocated to a trailer home in Memphis, Tennessee so the boys could be close to their father. In 1950, Mary and Arnold reconciled and remarried, moving the family to Pasadena, Texas. The marriage did not last, and they divorced for the final time in 1953. They remained friends, and the boys had regular contact with their father *(Olsen, 2001)*.

After the second divorce, Mary worked to support the family on her own, leaving the boys with sitters for extended periods of time. In 1955, she married Jack West, a traveling clock salesman, and had a third child with him. On the advice of a pecan nut salesman, Mary and Jack started a sweet business. The company was named Pecan Prince and was initially run from their garage. Dean and his brother worked full time operating the candy machines and packing the product. The candy was sold by Jack on his rounds, mostly in Houston, Texas.

Dean attended Vidor High School and, although he was regarded as a bit of a loner, did have social contacts and dated some girls. At an early age, Dean had rheumatic fever, which resulted in a heart murmur and prevented him from participating in sports. He was an average student and playing the trombone in the high school band.

In 1958, the West family moved to Houston to be closer to their main marketplace. Mary divorced Jack in 1963 and started her own sweet company, the Corll Candy Company. Dean was named Vice-President and his brother, Treasurer. When a male teenage employee complained about sexual advances from Dean, he was fired.

Dean was drafted into the United States Army in 1964, but after ten months of service, obtained a hardship discharge on the grounds that he was needed in the family business. He later stated that he grew aware of his homosexuality while in the Army. After he returned home, many people noted a change in his behavior, namely that he flirted with young males rather than females.

The Corll Candy Company moved to a location directly opposite Helm Street Elementary school in 1965. There Dean became known as the "candy man" for his habit of providing free candy to kids, especially teenaged boys.

In 1967, Dean Corll befriended one of the students from the school, 12-year-old David Brooks. Over the years, Dean became a father figure to David until he began paying the boy for sexual favors.

The Corll Candy Company declared bankruptcy in 1968, and Dean's mother moved to Colorado. He took a job as an electrician with the Houston Lighting and Power Company.

Crime Review:

Between 1970 and 1973, Corll is thought to have murdered at least 28 young men and boys between the ages of 13 and 20. Most of his murder victims were from Houston Heights, a predominantly low income neighborhood northwest of downtown Houston.

Corll's methodology was similar for all his killings. The victim would be lured into a vehicle owned by Corll or one of his accomplices. The victim would be taken to Corll's residence, where he would be drugged and tied to Corll's bed or a plywood torture board. He was subjected to sexual assault, torture, and beatings until he was either strangled or shot. The body was wrapped in plastic sheeting and buried at one of four places Corll had access.

Dean Corll's first victim was a University of Texas student, 18-year-old Jeffrey Konen. On September 25, 1970, Corll offered Konen a ride to his parent's home. His body was found buried at High Island Beach three years later.

Around the time of Konen's murder, David Brooks caught Corll in the act of sexually assaulting two teenage boys. In exchange for David's silence, Corll promised him a car. Corll later told Brooks the boys had been murdered and offered him $200 for each boy he would lure into Dean's clutches.

Between September 1970 and September 1971, a total of 10 teenagers were abducted and murdered:

- *December 15, 1970-* James Glass and Danny Yates, both 14. Brooks lured them away from a nearby religious rally. They were both raped and strangled. Their bodies were buried in a boat shed.

- *January 30, 1971-* Donald Waldrop, 15, and Jerry Waldrop, 14. The two brothers were walking to a bowling alley when Brooks and Corll lured them into a van. They were raped, tortured, strangled, and buried in the boat shed.

- *March 9, 1971-* Randell Harvey, 15. Last seen riding his bike to to his part-time job at a gas station. He was raped and killed by a single bullet to the head. He was buried in the boat shed, but his remains weren't identified until 2008.

- *May 29, 1971-* David Hilligiest, 13, and Gregory Malley Winkle, 16. Winkle was a former employee of Corll Candy Company. The pair were walking to a local swimming pool and last seen climbing into a white van. 15-year-old Elmer "Wayne" Henley, a lifelong friend of Hilligiest, offered to help distribute flyers to find the missing boys.

- *August 17, 1971-* Ruben Watson Haney, 17. He was walking home from a movie theater in Houston when Brooks convinced him to attend a party at Corll's apartment. He was raped, strangled, and buried in the boat shed.

- *September 1971-* Two more boys were murdered around this time, but their identities remain a mystery. One is known only as "Swimsuit Boy."

In late 1971, Brooks introduced Wayne Henley to Corll. Instead of adding him to his list of victims, Corll decided to make Henley an accomplice. He made the same offer of $200 per boy to Henley. Corll told Henley he was involved in a "sexual slavery ring" based out of Dallas.

At the beginning of 1972, Henley agreed to take Corll up on his offer because his family was in dire financial straits. Between March 1972 and June 1973, Henley and Brooks assisted Corll in the abduction and killing of at least 18 youths:

- *February 9, 1972*- William Branch, Jr., 17. He was lured into Corll's apartment with the promise of marijuana. He was emasculated, strangled, and buried in the boat shed. His remains weren't identified until 1985. His father, William Branch, Sr., a Houston police officer, died of a heart attack while searching for his son.

- *March 24, 1972*- Frank Aguirre, 18. He was a friend of Henley's and engaged to a girl named Rhonda Williams, who becomes important to this story at a later date. Brooks, Henley, and Corll approached Aguirre as he was leaving the restaurant where he worked, and invited him to hang out and enjoy a few beers and smoke marijuana. Aguirre was strangled and buried at High Island Beach.

- *April 20, 1972*- Mark Scott, 17. According to reports, Mark fought back against Corll as he was forced onto the torture board, but gave up when Henley held a gun to his head. He was raped, strangled, and buried at High Island. His body has never been recovered.

- *May 21, 1972-* Johnny Delome, 16, and Billy Baulch, Jr., 17. They were last seen walking to a local store. Baulch was another former employee of Corll Candy Company. Both boys were raped, strangled, and buried at High Island.

- *July 19, 1972-* Steven Sickman, 17. He was last seen leaving a party. He was bludgeoned with some blunt object, cracking several ribs, before being fatally strangled. He was buried at High Island. His remains weren't identified until 2011.

- *August 21, 1972-* Roy Bunton, 19. He disappeared on his way to his job at a shoe store. He was shot twice in the head and buried in the boat shed. His remains weren't identified until 2011.

- *October 2, 1972-* Wally Simoneaux, 14, and Richard Hembree, 13. Both were raped and strangled. Simoneaux managed to call his mother and shouted "Mama" into the receiver before the call was terminated. They were both buried in the boat shed.

- *November 12, 1972-* Richard Kepner, 19. Disappeared on his way to a phone booth. He was raped, strangled, and buried at High Island. His remains were identified in 1983.

- *February 1, 1973-* Joseph Lyles, 17. Lyles knew both Corll and Brooks, he and Brooks lived on the same street. He was strangled and buried at Jefferson County Beach. His remains were found in 1983, but not identified until 2009.

- *June 4, 1973-* William Ray Lawrence, 15. He was kept alive for three days, then strangled with a cord and buried at Lake Sam Rayburn.

- *June 15, 1973-* Raymond Blackburn, 20. A married man from Baton Rouge, Louisiana, who vanished while hitchhiking to see his newborn child. He was strangled and buried at Lake Sam Rayburn.

- *July 7, 1973-* Homer Garcia, 15. He was shot in the head and chest and bled to death in Corll's bathtub. He was also buried at Lake Sam Rayburn. Around this time, Brooks married his pregnant fiancee, leaving Henley and Corll to obtain victims on their own.

- *July 12, 1973-* John Sellars, 17. Killed two days before his 18th birthday. He was shot four times in the chest and buried at High Island Beach.

- *July 19, 1973-* Michael Baulch, 15. The brother of victim Billy Baulch, he was last seen on his way to get a haircut. He was raped, strangled, and buried at Lake Sam Rayburn. He wasn't identified until 2010.

- *July 25, 1973-* Marty Jones, 18, and Charles Cobble, 17. The two were abducted together. Cobble was a school friend of Henley's, and his wife was pregnant at the time of his murder. Both were shot and buried in the boat shed.

- *August 3, 1973-* James Stanton Dreymala, 13. Corll's final victim. He was out riding his bike collecting bottles to re-sell when he was abducted. He was raped, strangled, and buried in the boat shed.

On August 7, 1973, Henley targeted 19-year-old Timothy Kerley to be Corll's next victim. After smoking and taking drugs, they went back to Henley's home. They heard a commotion across the street where a drunk man was beating his teenaged daughter. The girl was Rhonda Williams, former fiancee of Frank Aguirre, whom Corll had murdered back in March 1972. Eager to get away from her violent father, Williams agreed to join Henley and Kerley. The three of them went to Corll's apartment together.

Initially, Corll was furious that Henley had brought a girl but eventually calmed down. He plied the teenagers with drugs and alcohol until they passed out. Henley awoke to find himself bound and gagged alongside Kerley and Williams.

Enraged, Corll informed Henley he was going to torture and kill all three of them. Henley managed to calm Corll and convinced him to release him if he agreed to help. Corll gave Henley a knife and told him to rape and murder Williams.

With Corll distracted with Kerley, Henley managed to grab Corll's .22 pistol. While Corll taunted him, Henley fired a total of 5 shots - one bullet hit Corll in the forehead but didn't pierce his skull, two more hit his left shoulder, and then three more in Corll's lower back and shoulder as he tried to flee.

Henley released the other teenagers, and they called the police. Henley confessed to his and Brook's involvement in the murders of dozens of teenage boys. Although the officers were initially skeptical, Henley provided enough details to persuade them there was substance to his wild tale. Brooks gave himself up shortly thereafter. Both accomplices gave full confessions and assisted in the recovery of bodies buried at the four different sites.

Henley compared the brutality Corll exhibited towards his victims as being "like a blood lust." He and Brooks instinctively knew when Corll "needed to do a new boy" because he would grow restless, chain-smoke cigarettes, and make reflex movements.

Henley and Brooks were tried separately. After various trials and retrials, both were sentenced to life imprisonment. Henley is currently in jail in Texas. Brooks died in May 2020 from COVID-19.

"Kill me Wayne, You won't do it!"

- Dean Corll's last words

Overview of Birth Chart

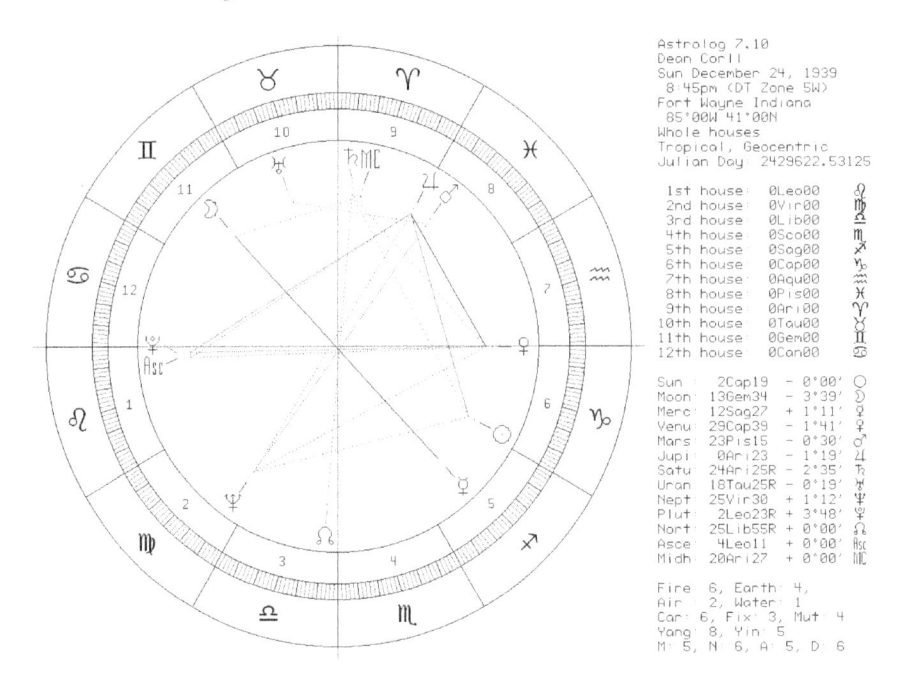

```
Astrolog 7.10
Dean Corll
Sun December 24, 1939
8:45pm (DT Zone 5W)
Fort Wayne, Indiana
85°00W 41°00N
Whole houses
Tropical, Geocentric
Julian Day: 2429622.53125

1st house:   0Leo00
2nd house:   0Vir00
3rd house:   0Lib00
4th house:   0Sco00
5th house:   0Sag00
6th house:   0Cap00
7th house:   0Aqu00
8th house:   0Pis00
9th house:   0Ari00
10th house:  0Tau00
11th house:  0Gem00
12th house:  0Can00

Sun :  2Cap19  - 0°00'
Moon: 13Gem34  - 3°39'
Merc: 12Sag27  + 1°11'
Venu: 29Cap39  - 1°41'
Mars: 23Pis15  - 0°30'
Jupi:  0Ari23  - 1°19'
Satu: 24Ari25R - 2°35'
Uran: 18Tau25R - 0°19'
Nept: 25Vir30  + 1°12'
Plut:  2Leo23R + 3°48'
Nort: 25Lib55R + 0°00'
Asce:  4Leo11  + 0°00'
Midh: 20Ari27  + 0°00'

Fire: 6, Earth: 4,
Air : 2, Water: 1
Car : 6, Fix : 3, Mut: 4
Yang: 8, Yin : 5
M: 5, N: 6, A: 5, D: 6
```

Dean Corll - December 24, 1939

Planets and points in the signs.

Leo Rising- He makes grand, over-the-top gestures, giving lavish gifts as a way to win people over. He is dramatic and loves to put on a show. He tends to intimidate others.

Sun in Capricorn- He is domineering and authoritarian, and comes across as cold, calculating, and unemotional.

Venus in Capricorn- He is selfish and has a strong desire to protect himself from being hurt. As a result, he becomes cynical and isolated.

Mars in Pisces- His masculine and feminine energies are in constant conflict. He feels the need hide your true nature. He is likely to experience emotional extremes, and can be impulsive, making rash decisions he later regrets. He lives in a fantasy world removed from reality.

Planets and points in the houses.

Mercury in 5th house- He is an excellent liar. He is highly creative and prone to exaggerate in order to get a bigger response from his audience.

Mars in 8th house- He is drawn to sexual taboos and has kinky preferences. He becomes obsessed with people in his life and demands absolute loyalty from friends and family.

Discussion:

Typical of earth signs like Capricorn, Dean Corll was efficient, concrete, and assumed a leadership role over his two young accomplices. True to his Leo rising, Corll showered his minions with extensive gifts, money, and cars in exchange for their blind loyalty. Perhaps the biggest clue in Corll's natal chart lies in his 8th house of sex and death, where Pisces brought a strong element of fantasy-fulfillment.

Because he was killed before he could be properly interviewed and analyzed, we will never know what Dean Corll's true motives were and what drove him down the path that became his life and epitaph.

Shared Pointers From the Natal Chart Reports

These two killers share a number of pointers in their Zodiac charts: Sun in Capricorn, Moon in Gemini, Venus in Capricorn, and Pluto in Leo. From these natal charts, it is apparent that both had a sense of being aloof from the world and lacking in empathy. In Shipman, this manifested in a mistaken belief he was rendering a service to the world. In Corll it became selfishness and catering to his own dark desires.

Chapter 11: Aquarius

(January 20 - February 18)
Modality- Fixed
Element - Air

Aquarius Personality Traits

Aquarians display the following positive properties:

- They are sociable and affectionate companions.

- Aquarians make faithful and trusted friends.

- They are independent and self-reliant, and do not rely on others to accomplish tasks.

- What you see is what you get; they are truthful and sincere in their dealings with all others.

- They are known for their compassion and helping others.

- Aquarians tend to be open to revolutionary ideas and ideals.

- They are generally clever and knowledgeable about different matters.

- They are innovative and prefer to work on projects that have humanitarian benefits.

But they can also exhibit the following negative attributes:

- Because they are revolutionaries, Aquarians can act contrary to and oppose generally accepted behaviors and processes.

- They are unpredictable and subject to change.

- They can be difficult to manage.

- Their clinical and impersonal personality may repel other people.

- They are aloof and dispassionate.

Despite being represented as the "water-bearer," Aquarius is actually the sign of <u>fixed</u> <u>air</u>. Aquarians are organizers and provide a stable structure and backbone to groups.

The air of Aquarius is like the jetstream that encircles the Earth, uniting everyone and everything. Those with Aquarius prominent in their birth charts have the unique ability to connect to every type of person and concept, no matter how abstract or foreign. The internet is an excellent analogy for Aquarius energy; it is an innovation that connects everyone, bringing people together from all over the world, for better and worse.

Aquarius Serial Killer 1: Gary Ridgway

Nickname: The Green River Killer

His nickname was given before he was caught because his earliest victims were recovered from the Green River near Seattle.

Biography:

Gary Leon Ridgway was born on February 18, 1949, in Salt Lake City, Utah, in the United States. His parents were Thomas Newton Ridgway and Mary Rita Ridgway. He was the second of three sons. He had a troubled childhood. His mother was overbearing and his parents would often get into violent arguments. She was physically and mentally abusive to her children and her husband.

As a child, Ridgway would torture animals; he once locked a cat inside a refrigerator until it died. He was a frequent bed-wetter until the age of 13. His mother would forcibly wash his genitals after each incident, belittling and humiliating him in front of the family.

Ridgway told psychologists he hated his mother but had conflicting sexual thoughts about her. He would fantasize about killing her. His father was a bus driver who often complained about the prostitutes along his route, which led Ridgway to have confusing feelings about sex workers *(Yancey, 2007)*.

Gary was dyslexic and struggled in school. His IQ has been assessed as being just above 80. After being held back a year, he finally graduated in 1969 and married his 19-year-old high school girlfriend. The marriage ended a year later because they were both having extramarital affairs.

At the age of 18, Ridgway enlisted in the United States Navy and saw combat in Vietnam. He frequently employed prostitutes, even after contracting venereal diseases on multiple occasions.

After marrying his second wife, Ridgway joined a local Pentecostal church and became devoutly religious, reading the Bible aloud at work, and canvassing from door-to-door. Despite his religious conversion, Ridgway still used the services of prostitutes. He and his wife had a son in 1975, but that marriage also ended in divorce.

Around 1985, Ridgway began dating Judith Mawson. He married for the third and final time in 1988. They were still happily married 14 years later when he was finally arrested. She was completely unaware of his violent double life.

According to all three wives, Ridgway had an insatiable sexual appetite, demanding sex multiple times per day. He forced his partners to engage in sex in public places, sometimes in areas where he would later hide his victims. He had a love/hate relationship with prostitutes. Some have theorized that his crimes resulted from being torn between his lust and devout religious beliefs.

Ridgway applied for a job as a police officer, but was not accepted. Instead, he found work as a truck painter in Bellingham, Washington.

Crime Review:

In 1963, at the age of 14, Ridgway tried to stab a 6-year-old boy to death, but the victim survived and the attack was never reported. He claims to have killed his first person as a teenager, by holding him underwater until he drowned, but this has been unconfirmed.

Ridgway started killing in earnest at the beginning of the 1980s. He is estimated to have murdered 71 women and teenaged girls around Tacoma and Seattle. He intentionally targeted women on the fringes of society, sex workers and runaways, knowing no one would notice if they went missing.

Ridgway planned and executed his killings carefully to confuse the police and avoid suspicion. He planted gum, cigarettes, and evidence belonging to other people with the bodies. This allowed him to evade police detection for decades.

He left clusters of naked bodies hidden in wooded sites around Green River and various "dump sites" in South King County. He would return periodically to perform necrophilia on them. Ridgway later claimed that he wasn't sexually aroused by the corpses, but having intercourse with them reduced his need for a living victim. It was one of the many ways he reduced risk and capture over the years.

The King County Sheriff's office formed a task force to solve the murders in the 1980s. Ted Bundy, in prison for his own murders, assisted the investigation by providing valuable insight into the mind of a serial killer. He suggested the killer was coming back to have sex with his victims, which turned out to be true.

Ridgway was almost caught several times. When the first bodies were discovered, he was considered a person of interest and brought in for questioning. He passed two polygraph tests, once in 1982 and again in 1986. In 1987, police took samples of his hair and saliva, but technology at the time was not sufficient to link him to the crimes. He remained free for another 14 years.

It wasn't until 2001 that DNA testing finally linked Ridgway to the 1987 homicides and he was arrested. He struck a plea bargain to avoid the death penalty. He confessed to 49 murders and agreed to show where he hid the bodies. He was sentenced to life imprisonment without the possibility of parole. Investigations revealed he killed at least 71 women, but the true number is probably much higher.

> *"I killed so many women, I have a hard time keeping them straight."*
>
> –Gary Ridgway

Overview of Birth Chart

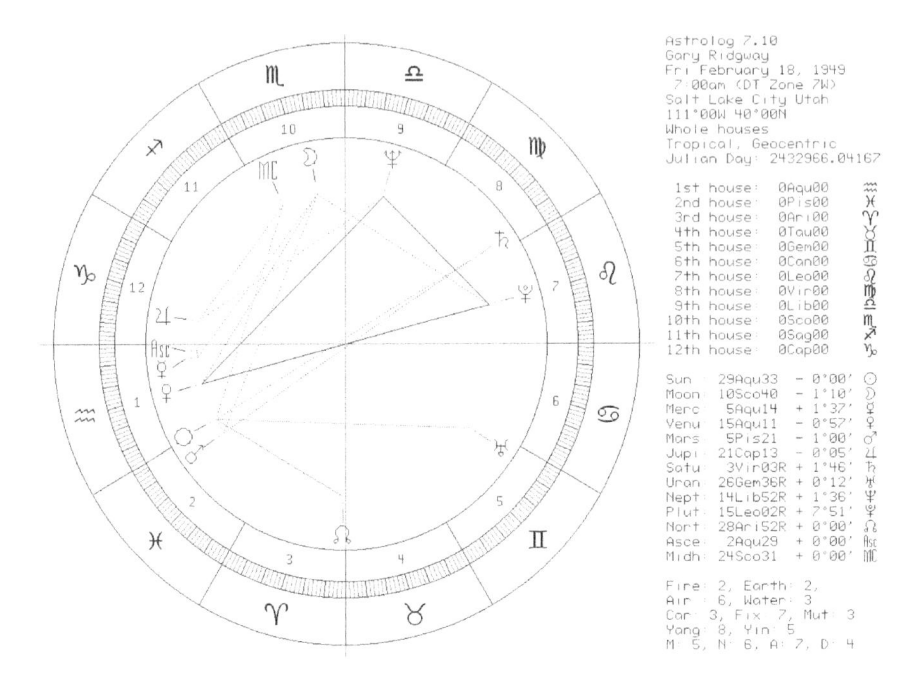

```
Astrolog 7.10
Gary Ridgway
Fri February 18, 1949
 7:00am (DT Zone 7W)
Salt Lake City Utah
111°00W 40°00N
Whole houses
Tropical, Geocentric
Julian Day: 2432966.04167

1st house:   0Aqu00
2nd house:   0Pis00
3rd house:   0Ari00
4th house:   0Tau00
5th house:   0Gem00
6th house:   0Can00
7th house:   0Leo00
8th house:   0Vir00
9th house:   0Lib00
10th house:  0Sco00
11th house:  0Sag00
12th house:  0Cap00

Sun   29Aqu33  - 0°00'
Moon  10Sco40  - 1°10'
Merc   5Aqu14  + 1°37'
Venu  15Aqu11  - 0°57'
Mars   5Pis21  - 1°00'
Jupi  21Cap13  - 0°05'
Satu   3Vir03R + 1°46'
Uran  26Gem36R + 0°12'
Nept  14Lib52R + 1°36'
Plut  15Leo02R + 7°51'
Nort  28Ari52R + 0°00'
Asce   2Aqu29  + 0°00'
Midh  24Sco31  + 0°00'

Fire: 2, Earth: 2,
Air:  6, Water: 3
Car: 3, Fix: 7, Mut: 3
Yang: 8, Yin: 5
M: 5, N: 6, A: 7, D: 4
```

Gary Ridgway - February 18, 1949

Planets and points in the signs

Sun in Aquarius- He is strong-willed and does not take emotional considerations into account. He may be unconventional, radical, and rebellious.

Moon in Scorpio- He is secretive by nature and has intense feelings. It is difficult for him to relinquish past hatreds and resentments.

Aquarius Stellium (Sun, Mercury, Venus)- He can be a rebel or trouble-maker and needs to express himself in unique, individualistic ways. Emotions do not sway his judgment and he doesn't let personal feelings get in his way. He needs constant change and can become bored easily.

Planets and points in the houses

Stellium in 1st house- The first house defines who he is. The excessive concentration of energy this house can create problems with self-control. He can be self-centered and self-absorbed. Everything must revolve around him.

Saturn in 8th house- He may have had an austere or abusive childhood. He is prone to phobia, anxiety, depression, and frustration. He is driven to explore taboos involving sex and death.

Neptune in 9th house- He can become fanatical about his beliefs and obsessed with religion. His quest for higher meaning can lead him down a false or misleading path.

Jupiter in 12th house- He may deny his own dark emotions, or not be able to handle the darker aspects of life. He has unrealistic expectations and turns to escapist fantasies to avoid the real world.

Discussion:

With a super-charged Aquarius stellium in his 1st house of self, Gary Ridgway was a paradox, with conflicting public and private personas. Caught in a tug-of-war between Saturn in his 8th house of sex and death, and Neptune in his 9th house of religion, it's easy to see how he became trapped in a vicious cycle of sex and righteous self-loathing. This led him to seek refuge in his 12th house of secrets and hidden places.

Ridgway's childhood resentment and hatred of his mother was projected onto his victims. His intense and secretive nature warped his emotional state, turning that hatred into an obsession.

Aquarius Serial Killer 2: Robert Christian Hansen

Nickname: The Butcher Baker

The nickname was coined by the media because Hansen's family ran a bakery business.

Biography:

Robert Hansen was born on February 15, 1939, in Estherville, Iowa, in the United States. His parents, Christian and Edna Hansen, were Danish immigrants. His father ran a bakery and Robert would later follow in his footsteps. His childhood wasn't easy; he worked long hours in the bakery under his strict and domineering father.

During his school years, Robert was the subject of ridicule and rejection. He was small and shy, suffering from severe acne that left deep scars on his face. He spoke with a stutter. Although left-handed, he was forced to use his right hand; the resulting stress made his stutter even worse.

He was shunned by the other kids in his school, especially the girls. He developed into a social outcast with a deep-seated hatred of women. He compensated by developing an interest in hunting and archery *(Gilmour & Hale, 2018)*.

In 1957, Hansen joined the United States Army Reserve and served for one year before being discharged. He became an assistant drill instructor at the Pocahontas Police Academy. He met a young woman and married her in 1960.

Crime Review:

In December 1960, Hansen set fire to a school bus garage as revenge for his miserable school years. He received a three-year sentence but was released after 20 months. During his prison time, he was diagnosed with bipolar disorder and had periodic schizophrenic outbursts. The psychiatrist who diagnosed him noted Robert was obsessed with getting revenge on people he felt had wronged him.

During his imprisonment, his wife of only six months divorced him. In 1963, he married his second wife, and they had two children. He was arrested numerous times for petty theft between 1963 and 1967.

The Hansens moved to Anchorage, Alaska in 1967, where they became respected members of the community. An avid hunter and sportsman, Hansen set several hunting records.

In December 1971, Hansen was charged with two separate crimes: the attempted rape of a housewife, and the rape of a prostitute. He received a five-year sentence but after serving only 6 months, was commuted to a work-release program and placed in a halfway house.

In 1976, he stole a chainsaw and was sentenced to five years' imprisonment. Even though his psychiatric evaluation found he was a danger to society, Hansen's appeal made it to the Alaska Supreme Court. They released him after he had served only one year. They didn't realize they were unleashing a killer back onto the streets of Anchorage.

Robert Hansen's murderous activities had begun years earlier, in 1972. At the time, Anchorage was a booming oil town, and the workers were flush with cash. Young women were lured north by promises of huge wages 'dancing' in clubs. With a steady stream of women arriving and leaving town, no one noticed if a few went missing.

Hansen's methodology consisted of luring a prostitute into his car and then abducting her at gunpoint to his cabin. There, he would rape her. If she was lucky, he would set her free when he was done, as long as she promised not to go to the police. The unlucky girls were flown out to a remote area in Hansen's private plane. There, he would release them into the wilderness and hunt them down like wild animals before killing them.

Hansen marked his aviation chart with Xs, showing the locations where he buried the bodies. A trophy collector, he saved jewelry and other mementos from his victims behind a false wall in his basement. It was this collection that ultimately led to his conviction.

On June 13, 1983, Hansen picked up a 17-year-old sex worker named Cindy Paulson. Kidnapping her at gunpoint, Hansen tortured, raped, and chained her by the neck to a post in his basement. He then drove her, in handcuffs, to his plane.

While Hansen was loading the plane, Paulson saw a chance to escape from the backseat of his car. Outrunning Hansen, she made her way to the highway where she flagged down a truck to take her to a hotel. The truck driver contacted the police, but Hansen convinced them the girl was trying to blackmail him. The police took the word of the mild-mannered baker over the prostitute.

Meanwhile, Alaskan State Troopers had been investigating the discovery of three bodies and what appeared to be one killer. They requested assistance from the FBI. Famed criminal profiler John Douglas was sent in to help.

Douglas theorized the killer was an experienced hunter with low self-esteem and a history of being rejected by women, who felt compelled to keep "souvenirs" of his murders. Upon learning of Hansen's hunting skill and lonely childhood, Douglas suspected he might be their killer.

On October 27, 1983, after searching Hansen's car, plane, and house, police found his hidden collection. Hansen was arrested and confessed to raping and assaulting over 30 women, of which at least 17 were killed. He was only officially charged with four murders, along with kidnapping and raping Cindy Paulson. He was sentenced to 461 years plus life in prison, without the possibility of parole.

Robert Hansen died on August 21, 2014, of natural causes.

Overview of Birth Chart

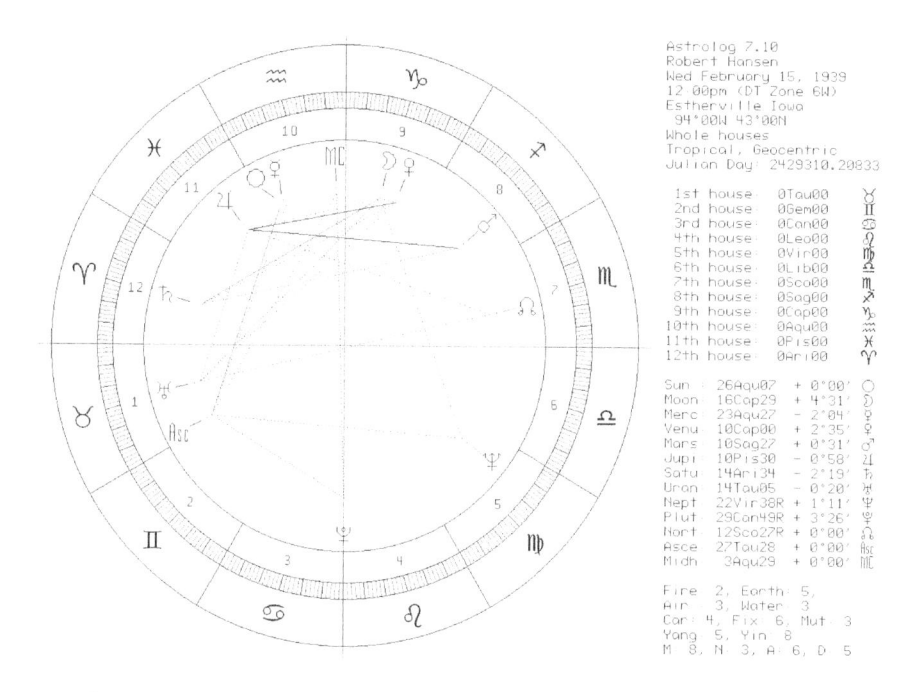

Robert Hansen - February 15, 1939

Planets and points in the Signs

Sun in Aquarius- He tends to become impersonal and rigid.

Moon in Capricorn- He wants to be revered and respected. He plans out every aspect of his life. He is fixated on keeping everything under control.

Venus in Capricorn- He has intense feelings and can become cold and calculating. He may come across as being aloof and detached.

Jupiter in Pisces- He prefers to withdraw from the harshness of reality into his own fantasy world.

Discussion:

Robert Hansen's path in life was shaped by the emotions of rejection and abuse from his childhood. He never forgave the girls in high school who rejected him, and with Jupiter in Pisces, he took those revenge fantasies to horrifying extremes. The presence of Aquarius and Capricorn in his chart helps explain his cold, calculating methodology and his need for respect within his community.

Shared Pointers From the Natal Chart Reports

Robert Hansen and Gary Ridgway share the Sun and Mercury in Aquarius. Both suffered from abuse and neglect in their childhood. These strong emotions from their youth became cold and calculating, twisting them into monsters.

Chapter 12: Pisces

(February 19 - March 20)
Modality - Mutable
Element - Water

Pisces Personality Traits

Pisces have many positive characteristics:

- They are ethereal and mystical, communicating otherworldly visions to mankind.

- Pisces have an instinctive understanding of other people's feelings.

- Their approach to others is sympathetic and caring.

- They are known for their compassion and empathy.

- Pisces are sensitive and always ready to respond to any actions or forces.

- They are inherently creative; many become artists or support artistic endeavors.

- Their kindness and sympathy can make them blind to faults in others.

Pisces traits can also become liabilities:

- They are dreamers and can lose touch with reality.

- They find it difficult to make up their minds and can easily be led astray.

- Pisces tend to float and go with the tide rather than accept responsibility.

- Communication is not a strong attribute; other people may see them as secretive.

- They may have difficulty formulating clear ideas, making it hard to understand them.

- Pisces are idealistic and always want to do everything correctly but often lack the determination to put it into action.

Pisces is the sign of <u>mutable</u> <u>water</u>. The water of Pisces is akin to the water molecules present within every living thing. Pisces has global awareness and is the most intuitive sign of the Zodiac.

They are the dreamers of the world and can create change through compassion and imagination. They are empathetic, but since they have the ability to feel collective pain, they may become overwhelmed and retreat inward as a way to cope.

Pisces Serial Killer 1: John Wayne Gacy

Nickname: The Killer Clown

He performed regularly at hospitals and charitable events as Pogo or Patches the Clown.

Biography:

John Wayne Gacy was born on March 17, 1942, in Chicago, Illinois, in the United States. His parents were John Stanley Gacy, a World War I veteran, and Marion Elaine Gacy, a homemaker. His family was of Polish and Danish descent and staunch Catholics. John had two sisters *(Kozenczak & Kozenczak, 2011)*.

John was close to his mother and sisters, but his father was a violent alcoholic who abused the rest of the family. He beat John unconscious on several occasions. Although his mother tried to protect him, that led to his father calling John a "sissy" and saying he "would probably grow up queer."

In 1949, a family friend starting molesting John. He never reported it to his parents for fear his father would blame him.

Obese and unrefined, John Gacy was bullied by kids at school and in the neighborhood. He suffered from a heart condition and several other maladies, which led to his frequent hospitalization. John's father accused him of faking his health problems for attention.

In 1962, John Gacy left home for Nevada where he worked as an undertaker's assistant and started to caress dead bodies. Gacy returned home terrified and shocked by his own behavior. He enrolled in Northwestern Business College and graduated in 1973. After graduation, he became a trainee manager with a local company in Chicago and, with hard work and discipline, was promoted and transferred to Springfield, Illinois.

In 1964, he married Marlynn Myers and joined the Springfield Jaycees, a non-profit organization dedicated to the development of management and leadership skills among young men. John Gacy worked hard for the Jaycees and rose to the rank of Vice-President.

His father-in-law purchased three Kentucky Fried Chicken (KFC) franchises. Gacy and his wife moved to Waterloo, Iowa in 1965 to manage the franchises. He established a club in his basement where his employees could drink and play pool. He only socialized with the young male employees. If one of them rebuffed Gacy's sexual advances, he would joke that it was just a moral test.

John's wife gave birth to a son in 1966 and to a daughter a year later. When his family came to visit, his father privately apologized for abusing him as a boy. John finally had the acceptance from his father he craved.

Gacy rose to be Vice-President of the local Waterloo Jaycees and served on their Board of Directors. Despite their outer appearance as a positive community organization, the Jaycees were heavily into pornography, wife swapping, drug abuse, and prostitution. Gacy found himself swept up into this dark lifestyle.

Crime Review:

In 1967, Gacy sexually assaulted Donald Voorhees, the 15-year-old son of a fellow Jaycee. Voorhees informed his father and Gacy was arrested. He paid one of his employees to rough up Vorhees to scare him, but it backfired; in addition to sodomy, Gacy was also charged with assault and intimidation. He pled guilty and was sentenced to 10 years in Iowa's State Men's Reformatory in Anamosa.

Following the sentencing, his wife filed for divorce. Angered, Gacy declared she and their two children were dead to him. He never saw his family again.

Gacy's father died from cirrhosis of the liver on Christmas Day, 1969. Devastated, Gacy requested compassionate leave to attend the funeral. His request was denied.

After serving 18 months of his 10-year sentence, Gacy was released for good conduct. He returned to Chicago, where he set about rebuilding his life and reputation.

On February 12, 1971, Gacy was charged with sexually assaulting a teenage boy, but the complaint was dismissed when the boy failed to appear in court. In June, he was charged with aggravated sexual battery on another boy, but that charge was dismissed after the youth attempted to blackmail him.

Gacy remarried in July 1972, but his second marriage didn't last long. His wife confronted him after finding gay pornography and questioned him about bringing teenaged boys into his garage. They divorced in 1976 on the grounds of marital infidelity.

In 1971, Gacy established a construction company, PDM Contractors. The business became so successful, he eventually quit his day job to manage it on a full-time basis. At PDM, Gacy employed only high school students and young men. He regularly insisted on sexual favors from his employees, either by threats or promising financial incentives or promotions at work.

Through his membership in a local Moose Club, Gacy began performing as a clown at fundraising events and children's hospitals. This would lead to the "Killer Clown" nickname that stuck with him after his murderous activities came to light. He was also active in politics and famously photographed with First Lady Rosalynn Carter.

In the period spanning 1972 to 1978, John Gacy killed at least 33 boys and young men, 26 of whom he buried in the crawl space of his house. He committed most of his murders between 1976 and 1978, when he was living alone after his divorce.

His victims were enticed by jobs at PDM, offers to drink and use drugs, money for sex, or simply grabbed by force. Gacy carried a sheriff's badge and would impersonate a police officer to lure victims into his car.

Once he brought his intended victim home, Gacy would ply him with drugs and drinks. His specialty was "the handcuff trick," in which he showed his guest how to escape from locked handcuffs. Gacy would demonstrate by freeing himself from the cuffs using a concealed key. He then invited the victim to try the game, and after handcuffing them, announce, "The trick is, you have to have the key."

With his prey confined, Gacy would proceed to rape and torture them. Inspired by Dean Corll, the Houston Mass

Murderer, Gacy devised different sadistic methods to enhance his enjoyment and sexual satisfaction. He typically murdered his victims using a rope tourniquet around their neck. He called this the "rope trick," and would tell his captive, "This is the last trick."

Gary would keep the body in his bedroom for a day or two, then bury it in the crawl space of his house. He poured quicklime over the corpse to aid in the decay process.

On December 11, 1978, Gacy went to a pharmacy to discuss a remodeling project. While there, he offered one of the employees, a 15-year-old boy named Robert Piest, a job working for him for more money. Before he vanished, Piest told a co-worker he was going to talk to "some contractor" about a job. Gacy abused, tortured, and killed him.

After Piest's disappearance, his family complained to the police. Gacy became the prime suspect and his house was searched. Although several suspicious items were discovered, there was not enough evidence to arrest him. The police placed Gacy under constant surveillance. Gacy joked around with the control teams, inviting them to join him for meals in restaurants and drinks in bars or at his home.

On December 18, Gacy filed a $750,000 civil suit against the police to stop the surveillance. A second search was conducted and officers noticed the smell of rotting flesh. On December 20, John Gacy finally cracked under the strain and confessed to his crimes.

Gacy was sentenced to death on a count of 33 murders. He was executed on May 10, 1994.

> *"A clown can get away with murder."*
>
> - John Wayne Gacy

Overview of Birth Chart

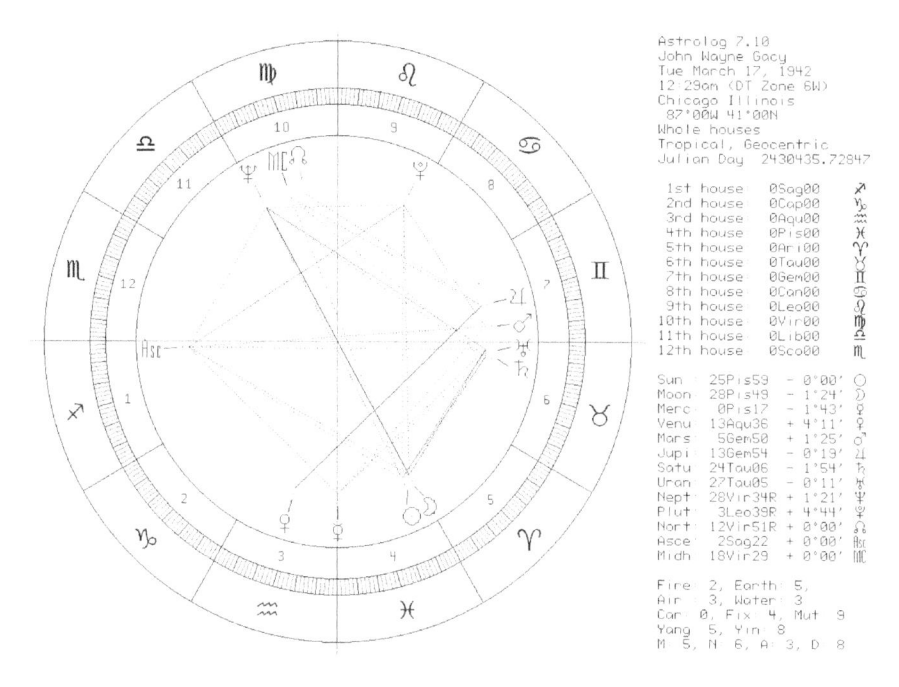

John Wayne Gacy - March 17, 1942

Planets and points in the signs

Moon in Pisces- He has an innate urge to withdraw from the demands and responsibilities of life. He may turn to drugs, alcohol, or other means of addiction as a form of escape. He tends to get lost in his own fantasy world.

Stellium in Pisces- He has heightened emotions and often retreats into the depths of his inner world to escape reality. He suffers from delusions, finding it difficult to separate the real world from his dream world. He tends to be a loner.

Venus in Aquarius- He dislikes rules he feels are too confining. He believes he is above normal social conventions. He can appear aloof and detached when interacting with others.

Mars in Gemini- He is impatient, argumentative, and may shoot off his mouth without thinking. He can be erratic, cynical, and rude.

Planets and points in the houses

Stellium in 4th house - He has a very strong connection to his family. His father plays a very important role in his life. Emotional imprints and conditioning from early in his childhood form the crux of his personality.

Jupiter in 7th house- He will marry well but his reckless behavior, including extra-marital affairs, can damage his relationships.

Discussion:

The key indicator in John Gacy's chart is the Pisces stellium in his 4th house of home and family. He was a sensitive boy who craved love and attention from his father, which he was denied. As an impressionable Pisces, the dark secretive world of the Jaycees, filled with drugs and pornography, was also a negative influence on him. This helped normalize the aberrant behavior that would later consume his life.

Pisces Serial Killer 2: Richard Ramirez

Nickname: The Night Stalker

The nickname was coined by the media because Ramirez operated in the dark.

Biography:

Ricardo "Richard" Leyva Munoz Ramirez was born February 29, 1960, in El Paso, Texas, in the United States. His parents were Julian Ramirez and Mercedes Ramirez, Mexican immigrants. He was the youngest of five siblings. His father had been a policeman in Mexico and was prone to fits of violent rage. To escape his father's temper, Richard would sleep in a local cemetery.

As a 12-year-old, Richard was strongly influenced by his cousin, Miguel "Mike" Ramirez. Mike was a decorated Green Beret veteran who fought in the Vietnam War. He boasted about his exploits, showing young Richard gory photos of his victims. In one picture, he posed with a woman's severed head. Mike taught Richard some of his military skills.

In 1973, Mike shot and killed his wife in front of Richard, spattering the 13-year-old boy with her blood. He was found not guilty by reason of insanity and committed to Texas State Mental Hospital. Richard became sullen and withdrawn after witnessing the murder, and moved in with his sister and her husband, Roberto. Roberto was a "peeping Tom" who would bring Richard along on his nocturnal activities.

Mike was released from the mental hospital after four years and resumed his influence over Richard. As a young teenager, Richard embraced sick fantasies of sexual abuse, rape, and sadistic behavior. He turned these into a belief system that led him to identify with Satanism *(Carlo, 2016)*.

Richard was a heavy drug user, including LSD. He dropped out of school in the 9th grade and moved to California where he started his killing foray.

Crime Review:

Ramirez used a variety of weapons ranging from handguns and a machete, to iron bars and knives. He was a sadistic killer who took pleasure in abusing, torturing, raping, and killing his victims.

His murder rampage lasted from April 1984 to August 1985. The killings showed no motive or common thread except for their brutality.

- *April 10, 1984-* San Francisco. Mei Leung, 9,. She was killed in the basement of a residential hotel. Her death wasn't attributed to Ramirez until 2009, when DNA evidence linked him to the crime. He had been staying at a nearby hotel.

- *June 28, 1984-* Glassell Park. Jennie Vincow, 79. She was stabbed repeatedly and her throat slashed.

- *March 17, 1985-* Rosemead. Dayle Okazaki, 34, and Maria Hernandez, 20. Okazaki was shot in the head at close range and died. Hernandez was shot in the hand, but the bullet deflected off her car keys. She survived.

- *March 17, 1985-* Monterey Park. Veronica Yu, 30. She was dragged from her car and shot several times.

- *March 27, 1985-* Whittier. Vincent Zazzara, 64 and his wife Macine, 44. Vincent was shot in the head. His wife was stabbed, her face mutilated. Ramirez carved out her eyes and took them with him.

- *May 14, 1985-* Monterey Park. Lillian and Bill Doi, 66. Bill was shot in the head. Lillian survived.

- *May 29, 1985-* Monrovia. Mable "Ma Bell" Bell, 83, and her sister, Florence "Nettie" Lang, 80. Keller was bludgeoned to death, and Satanic symbols were scrawled in various places. Both survived, but Bell later succumbed to her injuries.

- *May 30, 1985-* Burbank. Carol Kyle, 41, and her son, 11. She was sexually assaulted but survived.

- *June 27, 1985-* Arcadia. Patty Higgins, 32. She was sexually assaulted, strangled, and her throat slashed. Ramirez was later charged with her murder but the charges were dropped due to insufficient evidence.

- *July 2, 1985-* Arcadia. Mary Louise Cannon, 75. She was beaten and her throat slashed.

- *July 5, 1985-* Sierra Madre. Whitney Bennett, 16. She survived.

- *July 7, 1985-* Monterey Park. Joyce Lucille Nelson, 61. She was bludgeoned to death and mutilated.

- *July 7, 1985-* Monterey Park. Sophie Dickman, 63. She was sexually assaulted but survived.

- *July 20, 1985-* Sun Valley. Somkid and Chainarong Khovananth, 32, and their son, 8. Chainarong was shot to death. His son and wife were both sexually assaulted but survived.

- *July 20, 1985-* Glendale. Max, 68, and Lela Kneiding, 66. Both shot to death in bed as they slept.

- *August 6, 1985-* Northridge. Virginia and Chris Peterson, 38. Virginia was shot in the face. Chris was shot in the temple. Luckily for them, the ammunition was defective. Both survived.

- *August 8, 1985-* Diamond Bar. Sakina and Elyas Abowath, 35, and their son. Elyas was shot while sleeping. Sakina was brutally beaten, but she and her son both survived. After this attack, police announce they are after a serial killer. The press give Ramirez the nickname, "The Night Stalker."

- *August 18, 1985-* San Francisco. Peter Pan, 66, and his wife, Barbara. Peter was killed and Barbara was badly beaten and shot. She survived her injuries and was able to identify Ramirez from police sketches taken from the earlier survivors.

- *August 24, 1985-* Mission Viejo. Inez Erickson, 27, and Bill Carns, 29. Bill was shot in the head three times. Inez was sexually assaulted. Both survived. As Ramirez drove away, Erickson got a good look at his car, as did a local teenager who took down the license plate number.

On August 30, police found the car abandoned. Ramirez had wiped it for fingerprints but missed a single print on the rearview mirror. From it, police were able to identify him.

His mug shot aired on national TV and was printed on the front page of every major newspaper in the state.

Ramirez was unaware he'd been discovered until he walked into an East Los Angeles liquor store and saw his face on that day's paper. He panicked as the other customers realized who he was, calling him "*el matador*" ("the killer").

He ran away, crossing a busy freeway on foot. He was attempting to carjack a woman when a swam of angry locals surrounded him. They were in the process of beating him with a metal bar when the police showed up and arrested him. The 'Night Stalker' had finally been captured.

At his first court appearance, Ramirez raised a hand with a pentagram drawn on it and yelled, "Hail, Satan!" His trial lasted a year and was almost derailed during deliberations when one of the jurors was murdered by her boyfriend.

Ramirez was ultimately convicted of 13 murders and sentenced to death. While awaiting execution, he died of liver failure on June 7, 2013.

"We've all got the power in our hands to kill, but most people are afraid to use it. The ones who aren't afraid, control life itself."

– Richard Ramirez

Overview of Birth Chart

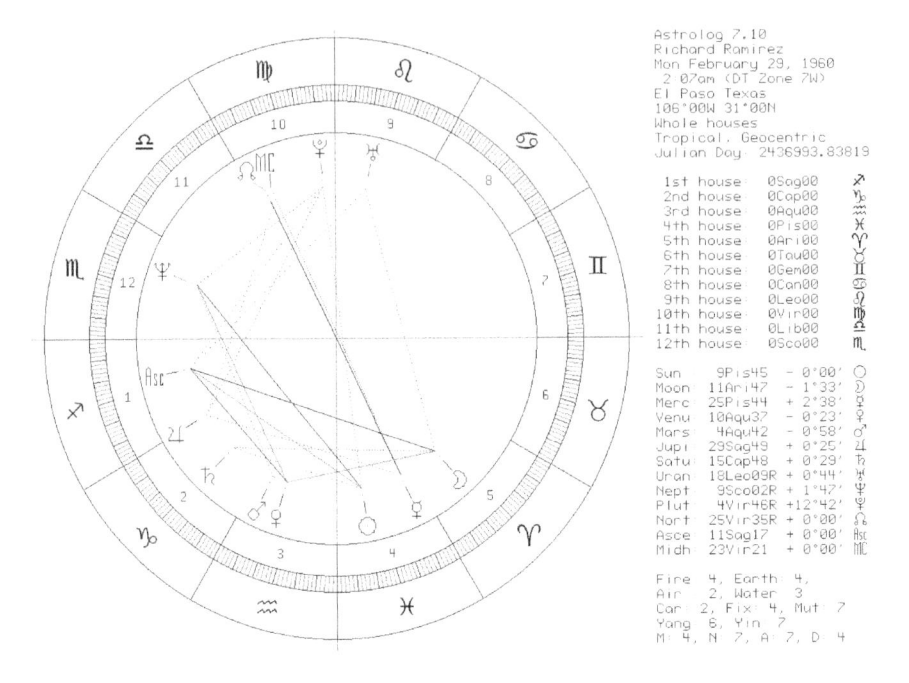

Richard Ramirez - February 29, 1960

Planets and points in the signs

Mercury in Pisces- He can be disorganized and overlook small details.

Mars in Aquarius- He has a superiority complex. He has his own unique sense of logic that makes him feel that he is right, no matter what.

Jupiter in Sagittarius- His life is filled with exaggerated extremes, including inappropriate self-confidence and demands for endless pleasure.

Planets and points in the houses

Jupiter in 1st house- He has an inflated sense of self, putting his wants and desires ahead of anyone else.

Sun in 4th house- Family is of great importance to him, and his parents were an enormous influence when he was growing up. He may have had a difficult childhood and a problematic relationship with a domineering father.

Moon in 5th house- He is driven by his own wants and pleasures. He is drawn to risk-taking behavior, such as gambling or thrill-seeking. He tends to leap before he looks.

Neptune in 12th house- He may have felt lonely and isolated from his peers, especially in his youth. He is inclined to escape into his own private fantasy world when life gets too harsh. He has addictive tendencies.

Discussion:

Richard Ramirez's Sun in the 4th house of family demonstrates what an over-sized impact his relatives, especially his male relatives, had on his life. Growing up, he didn't have a single positive male role model. As an adult, he combined the worst traits of all his childhood influences. Neptune in his 12th house of secrets helps explain his addiction to drugs as well as his sick, demented fantasies.

Shared Pointers From the Natal Chart Reports

John Gacy and Richard Ramirez share a Sun and Mercury in Pisces in the 4th house of family. They were both highly sensitive, impressionable young boys who were exposed to horrible abuse and atrocities at an early age. The childhood trauma left them with deep, lingering scars they could never outgrow. Without a positive influence to turn to for support, the negative aspects of their natures completely dominated their values and outlook on life.

Conclusion

This has been a sordid journey through the mindsets of 24 notorious serial killers from all over the world. They came from different cultures, backgrounds, and decades. Was there anything in their astrological natal charts that might have indicated the dark path their lives would take?

Of the 24 individuals studied, 14 contained one or more stelliums in their chart. This is not surprising, but it's also not an indicator of criminal behavior. Many high-profile businessmen, athletes, and celebrities have stelliums. It just means they put their hyper-intense focused energy to more productive use.

This raises the question of nature versus nurture. At best, the criminals in this book were neglected as children. At worst, they were subjected to some of the most horrific abuse imaginable. As a result, they started out life with a distinct disadvantage. If they were raised in a more balanced, loving environment, would they have projected the positive attributes of their signs, instead of the negative? Alas, we'll never know.

This brief excursion has provided some clues, but the sample size is too small to draw definitive conclusions. We will continue this investigation in future volumes and see what the stars reveal.

In closing, it's important to reiterate that astrology does not cause human behavior to manifest. It simply reflects possibilities, like a giant mirror in the sky. We still have free will. What we do with our time on Earth is up to us. Choose wisely.

References

Bardsley, M. (2006). *Angelo Buono*. Crime Library; Courtroom Television. http://www.crimelibrary.com/serial_killers/predators/stranglers/angelo_5.html

BBC News. (2000, June 14). Bomber "had abnormality of the mind" [News]. BBC.

Carlo, P. (2016). Night Stalker : The Life and Crimes of Richard Ramirez. Kensington Publishing Corporation.

Cunningham, Donna (2011). The Stellium Handbook: An Owner's Manual For People With Stelliums or Triple Conjunctions. Part One of Two.

Curtis, G. (2007, October 27). *Only in Oklahoma: Black widow enjoyed the limelight*. Tulsa World. https://tulsaworld.com/archives/only-in-oklahoma-black-widow-enjoyed-the-limelight/article_72d236aa-b108-5a0f-bec7-d21e5197193d.html

Dvorchak, R. J., & Holewa, L. (1992). Milwaukee Massacre : Jeffrey Dahmer and the Milwaukee Murders. Hale.

Farr, L. (1993). *The Sunset Murders*. Pocket Star Books.

Fawkes, S. (2004). *Natural Born Killer*. John Blake.

Frank, G. (2018). *The Boston Strangler*. Open Road Integrated Media.

Frasier, D. K., & Newton, M. (2007). Murder cases of the twentieth century : biographies and bibliographies of 280 convicted or accused killers. Mcfarland & Company, Inc.

Fuchs, C. (1996). *Bad Blood*. Creation Books.

Gilmour, W., & Hale, L. E. (2018). Butcher, Baker : A True Account of a Serial Murderer. Open Road Media.

Guinn, J. (2014). Manson : The Life and Times of Charles Manson. Simon & Schuster Paperbacks.

Hendorson, J. (1998, June 28). Henry Lee Lucas able to confuse authorities and then beat death. *Houston Chronicle*.

Hewitt William W. (2016). Astrology For Beginners : An Easy Guide To Understanding & Interpreting Your Chart. Llewellyn.

Joanna Martine Woolfolk. (2013). The Only Astrology Book You'll Ever Need. Taylor Trade Publishing.

Kaplan, R. M. (2010). Medical Murder : Disturbing Cases of Doctors Who Kill. Summersdale.

Klausner, L. D. (1981). Son of Sam : Based on the authorized transcription of the tapes, official documents and diaries of David Berkowitz. Mcgraw-Hill.

Kozenczak, J. R., & Kozenczak, K. M. (2011). The Chicago Killer : The Hunt for Serial Killer John Wayne Gacy. Xlibris.

Lindberg, D. C., Numbers, R. L., & Porter, R. (2003). *The Cambridge History of Science*. Cambridge University Press.

Miller, S. (2013). Nobody's Women : The Crimes and Victims of Anthony Sowell, the Cleveland Serial Killer. Berkley; London.

Montaldo, C. (2004, July 21). *Mass Murderers, Spree and Serial Killers*. ThoughtCo; ThoughtCo. https://www.thoughtco.com/defining-mass-spree-and-serial-killers-973123

Montaldo, C. (2019). *Profile of Serial Killer Derrick Todd Lee*. ThoughtCo; DotDash Publishing. https://www.thoughtco.com/derrick-todd-lee-973096

Montolli, E. (2017). *La seconda vita del ragionier Donato Bilancia, professione serial killer*. GQ Italia. https://www.gqitalia.it/underground/2017/05/29/la-seconda-vita-del-ragionier-donato-bilancia-professione-serial-killer

Olsen, J. (2001). The Man With the Candy : The Story of the Houston Mass Murders. Simon & Schuster (P.

Olsen, J. (2008). The Happy Face Killer. John Blake.

Orion, R. (2020). *Astrology for Dummies*. John Wiley & Sons, Inc.

Rickall, C. (2007). Yorkshire's Multiple Killers: Yorkshire Cases c. 1915–2006. Casemate Publishers.

Root, N. (2011). Frenzy! : Heath, Haigh & Christie : The First Great Tabloid Murderers. Preface.

Rose, D. (2011). The Big Eddy Club : The Stocking Stranglings and Southern Justice. New Press.

Sullivan, K. M. (2020). BUNDY MURDERS : A Comprehensive History. Mcfarland.

Vronsky, P. (2004). Serial Killers : The Method and Madness of Monsters. Berkley Books.

Yancey, D. (2007). The Case of the Green River Killer. Lucent Books.

Printed in Great Britain
by Amazon